Safety With Horses

Safety With Horses

Brian Giles
Cartoons by Jake Tebbit

Stanley Paul
London Melbourne Sydney Auckland Johannesburg

Stanley Paul & Co. Ltd
An imprint of the Hutchinson Publishing Group
17–21 Conway Street, London W 1 P 6 J D

Hutchinson Group (Australia) Pty Ltd
16–22 Church Steet, Hawthorn, Melbourne, Victoria 3122

Hutchinson Group (N Z) Ltd
32–34 View Road, PO Box 40-086, Glenfield, Auckland 10

Hutchinson Group (S A) Pty Ltd
P O Box 337, Bergvlei 2012, South Africa

First published 1985

© Brian Giles 1985
Illustrations © Jake Tebbit 1985

Set in 10/11 ½ pt Compugraphic Baskerville

Printed and bound in Great Britain by Anchor Brendon Ltd
Tiptree, Essex

ISBN 0 09 160481 8

Contents

Acknowledgements

My thanks to Jake Tebbit for his wonderful cartoons, Peter Roberts for his excellent instructional pictures, Marion Paull for editing the manuscript and Judith Draper for reading and checking the material. A special thank you, too, to all those people who work hard to make riding safer for children.

Peter Roberts' photographs were taken at the Belmont Country Club & Equestrian Centre, London NW7 and the Frith Manor Livery Stables, London N12.

Introduction

If you want to enjoy a life with horses and ponies, the only way to do it properly is to make it safe for both you and your mount. Too many accidents are caused by people being thoughtless and endangering themselves and the animals they love so dearly.

The reason for writing this book is to try and help you understand the risks involved in riding horses and ponies, or looking after them. And there is a key factor to it all: if you want to be safe, and keep your mount happy and well, you must think about what you are doing at all times. The password is commonsense.

Horses and ponies are among the loveliest creatures on earth; they serve willingly and, if treated with the respect they deserve, without question.

However, there are people who, for reasons best known to themselves, merely use them as a means of transport, just as they would a bus, or a car. What they forget is that the equine is not a machine. Horses and ponies have feelings, just like you; and, because they have, they can be hurt. So treat them well.

They also trust without question, so it is your responsibility to make certain that you look after their interests, as well as your own. Be foolhardy and fail to concentrate on what you are doing and you will be riding for a fall.

The fact is, though, you do not need to be riding a horse or pony to be hurt. Accidents can also happen while you are simply grooming, or leading, and you must exercise caution at all times. I do not mean to the extent that it destroys your pleasure, but just enough to be sensible, so that you cut down the risks for you and your horse. In other words, *think* and be safe.

1
Riding on roads

The first thing to remember when riding on roads is that the majority of drivers do not know anything about horses and, as a result, they will sometimes make mistakes. It can be a major problem for you, but it is one you must try to overcome by thinking for them and being sensible, even if you are seething because of their ignorance.

If ever you encounter difficulty on the roads, always remember to stay calm, because your horse or pony will rely on you totally. If you panic, you will transmit your fears to him and he could become over-excited and do something silly. He will not mean to do anything bad but, because he does not think or reason as you do, things could go terribly wrong.

To make everything easy for the drivers you meet on the roads, always ensure that you indicate your intentions clearly by using the correct signals.

If you are riding along a busy road, and you want to turn right, wait until a gap appears in the traffic, put your right arm straight out and ease your way across. Never shoot your arm out and simply start turning, assuming that everything will be fine, because it will not. You might not only hurt yourself and your horse, but a car driver as well. So always think quickly, clearly and be right.

To make a left turn, put your left arm out straight so that it is level with your shoulder and proceed to make the turn.

Should you need to ask traffic to slow down, extend your right arm horizontally and move it up and down slowly from shoulder height to waist level. But always bear in mind that this is not a command, merely a request for the traffic to comply with your

Don't use confusing hand signals

wishes. That is why you must not take anything for granted before moving out into the middle of the road, or stopping. If the motorist is ignorant of or misinterprets your signals, he might go charging past – you must always be prepared for that to happen.

Accidents generally occur when people in cars are late for work, or an appointment. Because they think that a horse or pony is like a motorized vehicle, they believe it will stop, turn or get out of the way when you want it to. As you know, this is not the case. A horse is a sensitive animal who can become very frightened; he might suddenly decide to shy away from traffic, or walk off a straight line into its path. That can prove highly dangerous.

It must, however, be pointed out that accidents on roads are not always the fault of drivers, many of whom do slow down when they have to pass someone out riding. A slovenly attitude on your part, or a silly mistake because you are not concentrating, can also cause an accident or, at the very least, a lot of bad feeling.

Never let your horse amble along on a loose rein and *never, ever, canter or gallop on roads*. Apart from the danger of running into something, your horse might slip and fall over, causing terrible injuries to himself and to you. Be sensible, only walk or trot, and always be in complete control of the horse and the situation.

If, for whatever reason, you have to stop oncoming traffic, raise your right arm, with the palm of your hand facing forward, just as a policeman does when he wants somebody to halt. When it is safe for the traffic to proceed, thank those you have held up by touching your riding cap, or nodding your head at the drivers and smiling. Make sure they see you say thank you. Always be polite and courteous because good manners go a long way and you need the co-operation of those who drive.

Behave as though you own the road – or are vastly superior to anyone else because you are sitting on a horse – and forget common courtesy, and you will find you are doing yourself and all other riders a disservice. There is never any excuse for bad manners. And, if *you* show a complete lack of interest, why should anyone bother to help you?

In order to wave traffic on, extend your arm and rotate it anti-clockwise in a semi-circular movement – be positive with every gesture you make, and yet not like a catherine wheel that has just been lit and is gathering speed. Remember that sudden movements can frighten horses and, as you have only one hand on the reins when signalling, the last thing you want is for your mount to start diving all over the place.

When riding on roads with several other people, always keep at least two horses' lengths away from the one in front of you. This gives your mount plenty of room in case the horse preceding you suddenly stops. Riding nose to tail or rushing your mount up behind the one in front can be dangerous. If the one in front happens to kick out, your horse might take a hefty, unnecessary wallop, which will hurt or even lame him.

Never ride several abreast on the public highway – it is extremely stupid, could lead to a lot of trouble and is a complete abuse of the road and the other people using it. If you must ride abreast, and I do not recommend it, the total number should be two; and you should only do so if one horse is inexperienced and the one on the outside knows what being ridden on the roads, in traffic, is like. Think safety all the time and consider your horse and other road users.

When riding with others do not hold continuous conversations; it is distracting and will prevent you from concentrating on what you should be doing. Be aware of what is going on around you at all times and you will arrive at your destination safe and sound. Remember, motorized vehicles do not have feelings, and cannot be hurt; but you and your horse can, and only if you know what you are doing at every moment can you be safe.

Some riders like to canter or gallop along the green verges which flank many of the roads in this country, but although it is fun to do so, I would not advise you to try it. When cars are travelling at speed, they need plenty of time to stop. If you fall from your horse, or for some reason he gets loose, he could be run into and not only be badly injured himself, but also cause an accident, injuring innocent people. You may think you can sit firmly on any horse, and that you are the best rider since triple Olympic gold medallist Richard Meade, but believe me, you are not – you can fall off as sure as night follows day.

Maybe, with a great deal of luck, you might be able to hold onto the reins if you fall, and so prevent the horse from galloping off into the traffic. But it is not likely; the chances are you will fall badly, or awkwardly, and not be physically able to cling on to the reins. So do not rely on good fortune, but always think ahead; do not gallop on road verges – in fact, if you can possibly avoid them in the first place, do.

Certainly it is delightful to gallop fast – the excitement is exhilarating – but it is all a question of doing the right thing at the right time, and not taking unnecessary, irresponsible chances. Where horses are concerned, there is always a clear, logical reason for not doing many of the things you would like; a moment of careful thought and consideration for the horse, and you can soon work out what is right and what is wrong and avoid any problems.

Many horses and ponies are used to the noise made by traffic and the dreadful smells sometimes emitted by the combustion engine. But those who are not can easily be frightened by lorries, buses and those hideous looking transporters which carry half a dozen cars mounted on their backs. If you know your horse is not 'bomb proof', try not to ride him on busy roads or, if you really must, make sure you have someone else riding with you whose mount is safe, so that you can keep on the nearside of them. The other horse will be a calming influence and, if your mount does become excited, you will be protected by the out-rider, and your horse will be unable to leap sideways into the traffic. This, however, as I have already mentioned, is the only time that I would recommend riding two abreast.

So far I have been writing mainly about riding on busy roads, where much heavy traffic is often encountered; but there are hidden dangers lurking on all roads throughout Britain, particularly on narrow roads and lanes in the country. On some of these quieter byways you might think you are safe, and in many cases you might well be, but always exercise extreme caution.

For example, remember that away from major towns the speed limit for motorized vehicles is sometimes lifted and so, what traffic you do encounter may be going much faster than you might expect. It can be particularly hair-raising if there are twists and sharp turns on the road.

The trickiest part of riding along narrow lanes is that there is very little room for manoeuvre, and taking quick evasive action can sometimes prove very difficult. The only thing to do is to be super alert at all times. On such lanes never ride two abreast but in single file, giving the leader plenty of space to come back if he has to in an emergency. And always walk round blind corners.

Even without the hazards of traffic, there are still many problems involved in simply walking or trotting a horse on the roads or lanes. Walking your mount downhill, for example, can prove difficult if the roads are covered with wet leaves. And nearly all roads have a camber, which means the surface slopes away slightly from its central point; what you must do is try and keep towards the nearside edge, so that at least the horse's left feet are on level ground and he can keep himself balanced. If you ride continually on the camber you expose him to more chances of slipping and sliding, which is not only uncomfortable for him, but could also be dangerous for you. Wet leaves on a flat surface are not too much trouble to cope with because the horse is always on an even keel. Your mount should wear knee boots so that if he did fall or stumble, they would protect him and his knees would not be grazed or cut.

What I would not advise you to do is to ride on roads or lanes when there is any quantity of ice or snow. The risks are obvious for your horse, but there is also another hazard: in icy conditions cars and lorries sometimes go out of control and a vehicle could career into both horse and rider, with terrible results. No matter how vigilant you may be there is very little you can do in such circumstances. The best thing is to stay away from road riding in bad winter weather or fog.

Even in good weather you should be aware that riding up and down hills needs care. Never allow your horse to amble along sloppily, but keep a good contact with his mouth and a firm knee and thigh grip on the saddle. When going downhill, sit vertical in the saddle, 'feel' the horse's mouth on your hands and let him use his neck to balance himself. On a steep uphill gradient shift your weight forward, have him on a longer rein and let him work his way forward at a pace that is comfortable for him. Do not pull at him, just go in rhythm with his movements and try actually to be a part of him as he strides forward. If the hill is very steep, get off and walk up it: it will do you and your horse good.

Riding in the country is always great fun, but bear in mind that in the autumn and winter months the light fades early, so again you must think about safety. You might not mean to stay out late but sometimes it will be beyond your control; or you might simply lose track of time, and find the dark closing in before you realize. So always make sure that you have the right equipment with you – reflective, fluorescent tabard and armbands and powerful stirrup lights, showing white in front and red at the rear.

At least these will give you some protection, enabling drivers to spot you, and giving them time to avoid running into you. But, of course, if you can avoid being out in the dark, or in fog, then do so, because no matter how many sensible precautions you take there is still a great deal of danger.

Even when you are riding on the roads in daytime it is advisable to wear a fluorescent tabard because it does make you that much more conspicuous. If you are a newcomer to riding, wear one which says 'Novice Rider' on it. You can also buy one that states the fact that you are on a 'Young Horse'. A lot of people have spent years working on ideas to make riding safer for you; so do take advantage of them, and invest in those items of clothing and equipment that really matter. Riding around looking like a coloured beacon is much better than not being able to ride at all because of injury.

Lights and tabards are not too expensive and can be bought at most tack shops. The proprietors will give you all the help you need. Just go in and ask how much things cost and someone will explain in detail how everything works. They will be only too pleased to help. It is good business for them, and very essential for you to know as much as you can about safety precautions.

In those far off days when traffic was only a fraction of what it is now, you might have been safe without all this equipment, but those times have gone forever, and it makes sense to take whatever precautions you can.

Sometimes you may have to lead your horse along the road. When doing so remember to keep to the left and to place yourself between him and the traffic. This means it is important to get him used to being led on the offside as well as the nearside which is the side from which horses are usually led. Never lead your horse with only a headcollar – he must wear a bridle because that gives greater control. In fact, it is against the law to lead a horse on the roads without a bridle.

The reins should be taken over the horse's head and your left hand should hold them only a short distance from the bit. Place your right hand firmly round the buckle end of the rein. Talk to your horse occasionally as you walk along. This will reassure him, and you.

Traffic is not the only hazard to be encountered when leading or riding horses and ponies; you must also be prepared for dogs to come bounding out at you, barking loudly. On many occasions they mean no' harm, but the shock of their sudden appearance can sometimes be very frightening. Be ready for this to happen and, if it does, pat your horse on the neck and talk to him. Some horses are not bothered about dogs, vociferous or otherwise, but some are and tend to leap about all over the place.

Ideally, everyone who rides horses should take a specially designed Road Safety test. The British Horse Society's Pony Club has a first rate test. Thousands of young people have taken and passed it with honours and are much safer as a result. For details contact your local branch of the Pony Club, or write to the Pony Club headquarters at the British Equestrian Centre, Kenilworth, Warwickshire CV8 2LR. They will give you all the information you need, but remember to enclose a self-addressed, stamped envelope for the reply.

Among other organizations to take road safety seriously is the London Borough of Bromley, who started a Road Safety scheme years ago, having recognized the fact that many people needed help and constructive advice when riding on roads. It was good planning on the part of all those involved. Their test, I might add, is free, so there is no excuse for riders in that particular area not to take advantage of this facility.

The test is in three sections under the following headings: Knowledge, Schoolwork and Roadwork. In the first part there are questions on police signals, motorist signals, maintenance or adjustments of tack, riding and traffic signs.

There are four tests in the second section: the first deals with the fact that you should make a thorough check of the condition and fitting of your saddlery, and the condition of the pony or horse and its shoes; then the rider should make sure that he, or she, has suitable clothing, including shoes or boots which cannot slip through the stirrup irons, and a hard hat.

In the second phase of the Schoolwork section all entrants are required to ride through a series of nuisances, which will include those they may encounter while riding out: loud noises, waving flags and other hazards designed to test the ability of the rider to cope with his/her mount under difficult conditions. It really is the only logical and practical way to find out if horse and rider are safe to be on the roads.

The third phase deals with mounting and dismounting; the rider is expected to do both as smoothly as possible, with an even feel on the reins, and the pony must not walk forwards or backwards during the exercise. The fourth test deals with leading, and approaching a hazard.

Most of these points I have already covered, as I have those in the Roadwork section of the Bromley test. This takes in starting – the rider must always look behind and give a clear right-hand signal before moving off – and also incorporates turning left and right, and riding in company. All good, useful information, which you must know if you are to be safe at all times.

If you are interested in taking a road safety test, and you certainly should be, write to your local Council and see if they run a scheme similar to the one in Bromley. Should your Council not operate one, they might be encouraged to do so if they receive enough requests – which would be good for all concerned.

The thing to remember is to *think* safe – and then you will *be* safe. It is all a matter of commonsense and concentrating hard on what you are doing. That, really, is the key to it all. Also, read and remember as much as you can on the subject – it will all come in useful at some stage.

Many safety tests require a rider to learn how to ride one horse and lead another, and I can understand it is a useful skill to acquire. But my advice to you is never to ride on public highways leading another horse or pony. There is enough involved controlling one mount – trying to cope with two is just an extra risk. If you have to take more than one horse somewhere, allow yourself plenty of time and make two journeys instead of one. It takes longer but, in my opinion, it is worth it in the long run. Or why not simply get some- one to help you?

It stands to reason that everything becomes more difficult when you have two horses to cope with. You only have one hand holding the reins of the animal you are riding, the other being on the reins of the led horse. What happens if you need to use either hand in an emergency? The answer is chaos, and perhaps a loose horse running about on the road. In my view, it is just not worth the trouble it may cause, nor the injuries you, the horses and drivers might suffer as a result of an accident. Remember, there is always a way around problems – though sometimes it does take a certain amount of planning beforehand.

Remember, too, to give way to people who want to use zebra crossings, and give pedestrians plenty of room in case your horse shies and careers into them. They could be hurt and might become terrified of horses and ponies for ever. They might also sue you if they suffer physical damage.

This is a good time to mention insurance because, if there is an accident, you could well be legally responsible, and that can sometimes cost a lot of money. Third party insurance is essential and you will find that it is not terribly expensive. Better still, if you can afford full cover, then have it because, in the long run, it can be well worthwhile. The best thing to do is to contact several insurance companies and get the best value possible. A good many firms now offer excellent cover for horse owners. Norwich Union, for instance, makes a point of offering riders insurance and will be only too pleased to give you any information you require. I had to make a claim from them over our family pony and the money came to me very quickly. That is the kind of good service you require.

They launched the Horse Plus, a package policy for horse, rider and tack, in 1973, and a number of improvements have been made since. The policy in the Horse Plus insurance covers, for the horse, death, permanent loss of use and loss by theft or straying: market value or sum insured; vets fees: up to £1,000 in any one year of insurance, with the policy holder bearing the first £50 of each occurrence.

Where an animal can no longer be used for its original purpose, the owner will not always want to have it put down, if it can live happily in retirement. The permanent loss of use cover under the policy will pay 100 per cent of the horse's value if it cannot be ridden. Where it can still be ridden, or used for breeding, 75 per cent will be paid. An amount of up to £100 will be paid towards the cost of advertising for lost or strayed animals and/or payment of a reward leading to recovery.

As for the rider, the policy states that accidental injury, causing death (as can so easily happen when riding on major roads),* loss of sight or limbs or permanent disablement: a sum of £5,000, and legal liability can be anything up to £500,000.

Tack is covered up to £500, with the policy holder bearing the first £15 of each occurrence. To give you an idea of what this costs, at the time of writing premiums range from £36 for a hack valued at £300 up to £135 for a hunter worth £1,500. The Norwich Union also offers a Selective Horse policy. If you want to know more about it, write to them at 1 Saint Stephens Street, Norwich NR1 3TA.

Of course there are many insurance firms which will cover horses, ponies, and equestrian equipment; it is just a matter of shopping around and getting the best possible value. To be really safe on the roads, and to save yourself a lot of financial trouble if things go wrong, you must insure both yourself and your horse, and be covered for third party, because accidents can so easily happen.

It is worth remembering, incidentally, that members and associates of the British Horse Society Pony Club are automatically insured against third party legal liability, up to £500,000, arising from their equestrian activities at all times for themselves and their ponies. All branch activities, which come under the umbrella of the Pony Club, are also covered. This is very good value indeed when you consider that subscription to the Pony Club is, at the time of writing, only £7.30 per year.

So, remember, since riding on roads can be dangerous, it is best to be covered by insurance at all times. It will make life much safer for you and your horse or pony, and you will be able to ride out with confidence and pleasure.

*My parenthesis

2
Rules before riding

Making sure that your saddle and bridle fit correctly before you go out on a ride is of vital importance. Failure to do these basic things properly can lead to dire consequences later on. The first rule to remember is never to be in a hurry. If you rush headlong into something you do not fully understand, you will make mistakes which might eventually lead to your hurting yourself or, at the very least, being given a fright.

When preparing to ride, always allow yourself plenty of time. All too often I have seen young riders dashing down to stables and, within minutes, they have thrown their tack on the horse or pony, and are trotting off down the road. Never behave like this: it is very dangerous, silly, and totally unfair to your mount. There are specific points to be checked before you leave the stables and failure to comply with the rules before riding will lead to a lot of trouble.

The first thing to do is to forget all you have been thinking about before visiting the stables, and, the moment you step into the loose-box, stall or yard, to concentrate your thoughts on the horse. Once you are with him, he is your responsibility, and there is no room for anything else in your mind. If you are not concentrating one hundred per cent, you will probably forget something vital to your safety in the saddle.

We will assume that it is summertime and that the horse you are riding is one who has been brought in from the field, given a small feed and is waiting for you to prepare him for the ride. The first thing to do is to fetch a headcollar from the tack room, go to his stable and secure him to the string loop attached to the ring in his stable, using a quick release knot (see Chapter 4 on tethering and leading). Then if the horse pulls back, he breaks the string, not the headcollar rope or the headcollar.

Once the horse has been secured, pick his feet out and remove the mud from the stable. If you leave it there, he will step on it and clog up his feet again. Pick it up and put it on the yard just outside the stable, where it can be cleaned up when the yard is being swept.

The next step is to go and get the rest of your grooming kit, which should consist of a body brush, rubber curry comb, dandy brush and a stable rubber, which looks something like a thick linen tea towel, and the hoof pick, which you have already used. If your hoof pick is not the type which folds up, always remember to put it back in the grooming kit or box and do not leave it in your pocket. The reason for this is that if you popped it in your pocket, then went riding and fell off, you could injure your leg. Always remember to put back equipment where it belongs after use – that way you will not make mistakes which could hurt you. In fact, tidiness around horses is of the utmost importance and is good training for you.

Before even attempting to put your saddle and bridle on, you must make sure that the horse or pony is comfortable, and that means giving him a good grooming so that he not only looks good, but feels that way, too. Horses do not think or react in the same way as we do, but they do know when they are not comfortable and if you leave them caked up with mud, or stable waste, when you ride out, they will not feel too good about it – and you will be seen by others to be lazy and not a fit person to be connected with animals.

I am a great advocate of tidiness, cleanliness and care with horses, and anyone who is not prepared to put in some hard work has no right to be anywhere near them. There are plenty of other pastimes or hobbies they could be involved with, which do not call for such dedication; those who are not willing to devote themselves to the animals in their care, or simply cannot spare the time, should leave well alone. There is no valid excuse for not doing the job properly. Only the truly keen and dedicated person stays with horses for any length of time.

It is, perhaps, even harder on those who love riding but cannot afford their own horse, because they do all the hard work knowing someone else is going to ride the animal whenever they like. Still,

Always carry your saddle properly

those who really care accept all that and still remain happy.

Now that you have your grooming kit, put it in the corner of the stable so that your mount does not bump into, or step on it. Use the rubber curry comb to rub the dried mud off his coat with a smooth downward hand movement, remembering always to go the way the hair lies and not against it. If you brush the hair in the opposite direction, it might upset him and, more important, if you brush the hair the wrong way, and then place a saddle on his back, it could cause soreness, which you must avoid at all costs. You can also use the stiff dandy brush to clean off mud, but not on the mane or tail or sensitive areas.

Once you have cleaned off the dried mud use the body brush, which has soft bristles, to rid the animal's face and body of any loose hairs left by the curry comb and dandy brush. As the bristles, which are closely knit, are much softer than the dandy brush, it is ideal for brushing the head, ears and tummy region. It feels good to the horse and, if you use it properly, he will remain content while you work. The body brush must also be used for cleaning the horse's mane and tail, again with downward strokes, to get rid of mud and to disentangle the hairs, which may have become entwined if he has been rolling in his field. After attending to the main parts of his body, replace the equipment used, then wash the horse's hooves taking care not to wet the sensitive heel area, and apply hoof oil. Not only does this make the hoof look clean and healthy, it also helps to promote horn growth.

Cleaning the hooves before riding also gives you a chance to check that the shoes are not loose. This is very important because if a shoe works loose, the horse can damage his feet by stepping on the nails with his frog (the V shaped rubbery substance in the hoof) or by puncturing the soles of his feet with them. There have even been cases in the past when a loose shoe has come off while a horse was being worked and hit somebody walking by. It is unusual, but it pays to be safe by checking the feet carefully before any horse leaves the stable area. In fact, the hoof is the most important part of the animal and if the feet are neglected, all sorts of complications can arise which take a great deal of time to put right.

Although all these checks to be made before actually riding out may seem boring, I cannot stress hard enough the importance of them. You may think, as far as the horse's feet are concerned, that as long as he is sound everything is fine. But failure to pick them out before and after a ride, or leaving his bed un-mucked out for long periods, could lead to a condition called thrush, which, though it can be cured, certainly highlights the fact that he has not been given proper care and attention. If your horse or pony does contract thrush, you have not been doing your job properly, and can be classed as neglectful, incompetent and unfit to be anywhere near stables.

The shoe check is also important for another reason: as I have already mentioned, oiling the hoof helps to promote growth of the horn and when the hoof grows it expands and the shoes can become too small for the horse. Just as a child, who has some new, well-fitting shoes, soon grows and needs another pair, so a horse will suffer pain and develop corns if his shoes are not changed regularly.

Another relevant point to note is that the clenches on shoes (the ends of the nails which are turned over to keep the shoe in place) sometimes turn up and stick out. This means that when the horse is walking, trotting, or in faster work, he could cut himself which, as far as I am concerned, is unforgivable. The shoes must be checked daily and if you find they are worn or loose, or the clenches need attention, summon the blacksmith at once.

To give you a guide, the shoes on a horse or pony who is working regularly on roads will need to be replaced with a new set at least every five or six weeks. (See Chapter 9 on picking up legs and cleaning feet.)

One of the advantages of keeping a mount at livery is that the blacksmith calls regularly. Nevertheless, the final responsibility for your horse's feet rests with you. Always remember my 'Rules before Riding' and you will not go far wrong. Disregard them, and you will be letting yourself and the horse down.

When you have groomed your horse and checked his feet it is time to change into your riding clothes, which should consist of a hard hat, jodhpurs, or breeches, jacket and riding boots. The hat should fit properly and have a safety harness attached to it (see Chapter 3 on protecting your head). The boots can be either long ones or the ankle length style.

The advantage of the long boot is that, as it comes up to just below the knee, it protects your leg and prevents it being rubbed by the stirrup leathers. I like this style of boot because, apart from the obvious advantages, it is suitable not only for everyday use but also for hunting, showjumping or showing. It may be made of leather, which is very expensive, or rubber, or some form of plastic. Whatever the material, long boots are worth having, although, like everything else, they must be looked after and cleaned regularly, if they are not to crack and become next to useless.

Many people have a habit of using the edge of a doorstep to remove their boots when they have finished riding, instead of using a boot jack, which has been specifically designed for the purpose. It may be much more convenient, but it is a bad policy, because everytime you put a boot into contact with concrete, it scuffs, cuts or weakens it and in no time at all you will find that the end nearest the heel splits open. While you could carry on riding in split boots, it would be uncomfortable and when it rained your feet would take a soaking. So protect your boots by using a proper boot jack.

An advantage of the short style riding boot is that it can be used as a dual purpose boot because, nowadays, it is very fashionable to wear this sort of footwear even when you are not riding. Short boots are of a very smart design, made of leather, and last a long time if they are cleaned regularly and kept in good repair.

But remember that all the good points about riding boots are wasted if you buy a pair which does not fit you correctly. If the boots are too wide, your feet will slip about in them and be uncomfortable, and if they are too small or narrow they will cause blisters, or corns. And never, ever, ride in boots which have been half-soled. They have a join across the area where the foot is in contact with the stirrup iron, and if you fell and the joined sole came apart from the upper, if could become entangled in the iron and you could be dragged.

When riding you need to be comfortable otherwise you will be thinking about things other than riding, and that can lead to mistakes which, in turn, might lead to accidents.

Some people do not wear jodhpurs or a jacket when they ride, but I do not recommend this. Jeans or trousers are not ideal because you can chap your legs when trotting, cantering or galloping and they do not look right. I have always believed proper riding equipment is far better and much smarter. Always look good and you will feel good.

Now that you have changed, it is time to go and fetch your tack and put the saddle and bridle on your horse. Some people do this as soon as the animal has been groomed, but I do not think it a good idea to leave a horse in a stable on his own, with a full set of tack on, as he might become frightened and get loose. Many horses and ponies are sensible and would just stand in their box and wait for your return, but some might brush up against the sides of the box and damage the saddle, or get tangled up in the bridle, no matter what precautions you take.

There is a case for putting just the saddle on, and leaving the bridle until you have changed. The horse has what is called a 'cold back' and putting the saddle on before you are ready to ride allows him time to get used to it before you mount. Although that is more acceptable, I still believe in sticking to my rules because then there is no room for accidents.

When you collect the tack, carry the saddle by placing it on your lower arm so that the pommel end is nestling up against your inside elbow joint, and place the bridle over your shoulder, with the reins looped up over the headpiece. If you are not comfortable carrying the saddle in this manner, hold the pommel top in the palm of your left hand and rest the underneath of the saddle against your body. That way the weight is resting in your hand and the saddle is, therefore, less uncomfortable to carry.

Always put the saddle on before the bridle, while the horse is still tied up and unable to walk round the box while you are organizing things. If you use a numnah (felt, leather or sheepskin), place it on the horse's back, but do not pull it taut and when you put the saddle on top of it make sure it is pushed up into the gullet of the saddle to avoid pressure on the spine. Let the girths of the saddle hang down on the offside. Once you have made sure that the saddle is fitting properly on the horse's back, walk round the front of the horse and arrange the girths so that they are hanging straight and are not twisted in any way. Always pass under the horse's neck – if you were to walk round behind him there is a chance that you might be kicked. Most horses, particularly in riding schools, are used to people walking close to them, but it is always best not to take chances because every horse or pony can have an off day and it might be the one time you are within striking distance.

Once you have made sure the girths are hanging correctly, return to the nearside, put your hand under the animal's tummy, take hold of the girths and secure them to the straps situated beneath the saddle flap. Before doing this, however, run a hand along his girth area to straighten out the hairs of his coat so that they are lying the right way. If they are not, when the girth is tightened and he goes out on his ride they may cause soreness. Once you have the girths in place tighten them so that the saddle will not slip, but do not pull them up too tight. Your horse may have a cold back, and a cold saddle pressing down on to it may cause him to kick out. He might also blow himself out with air. If he does, it will appear that the girths are tight; but, the moment he relaxes, you will find that they are fairly loose. So tighten them a hole at a time and, when you mount, pull them up again.

The saddle must always be fitted in such a position that, when the rider mounts, he/she will be as near as possible to the animal's centre of gravity. This helps the horse to keep his balance when working and does not put pressure on his spine. The saddle must never be too far back because, if it is, it will rest on the horse's loins and the rider's weight will make him uncomfortable and might even cause bruising or soreness. When the saddle has been fitted you should be able to see daylight when you look along its gullet. If your horse or pony has high withers, the underside of the saddle may press on them, which would cause cuts, bruising or soreness. One way to avoid such problems is to fit a numnah underneath the saddle which will take any pressure, and cushion your weight. If your animal is thin-skinned a foam numnah will be a great help because air can circulate beneath it.

Ignore these precautions, or fit the saddle incorrectly, and your horse could hurt his back – and that might mean he cannot be ridden for some time. Once the back is sore, or cut, scabs can form and if you attempt to ride the horse before they are healed you will knock the scabs off and have to start all over again. Taking the right precautions will prevent a sore back and ensure many hours of enjoyable riding.

Once the saddle is in place it is time to put on the horse's bridle. Hold it by the top and give it a good shake so that the leather is not twisted. Then undo the headcollar, slip it off his nose, slide it down to his neck and refasten the buckle. This leaves his head free in order for you to fit the bridle, yet prevents him walking off while you are working.

Fitting the bridle correctly is most important. You must be very gentle and patient when doing it, otherwise you might frighten the horse, bang the bit up against his teeth and put him off the whole exercise forever. Avoid that at all costs, otherwise life for you both will become very difficult. Place your right arm underneath the horse's jaw and hold the top of the bridle. With the other hand holding the bit encourage him to open his mouth by pressing gently on the outer edge of his mouth with the thumb of your left hand. When the mouth opens, carefully insert the bit and then slip the headpiece over the top of his head so that the ears are between the brow band and the headpiece of the bridle. Arrange his forelock so that it lies over the brow band.

Having accomplished this, make sure the bridle fits, and particularly that the bit is neither too high nor too low in his mouth. Next, fasten the throatlatch. It should be tight enough to prevent the bridle slipping over the horse's ears, but not too tight – you should be able to insert four fingers between the bottom of the throatlatch and his throat. Fasten the noseband, making sure it is inside the cheek pieces. It should lie just below the horse's prominent facial bones, and when fastened you should be able to insert two fingers between it and the horse's jaw. Once this is done, release the headcollar, hold your horse by the reins, undo the stable door and push it right back to give your horse a clear area through which to walk. Before you take him out ensure that the stirrup irons are run up their leathers or crossed over the saddle, so that they do not bang against anything, or get caught up in the door as you move off. Never allow the animal to rush through the doorway, or to go through at an angle. Take him slowly, quietly and straight, and talk to him all the time. (See Chapter 4 on tethering and leading.)

Once you have left the stable, make a quick check to see that everything is in order and you will then be ready to ride.

3
Protecting your head

I believe that the wearing of riding hats, like car safety belts, should be made compulsory. I cannot see any logical reason for not doing so. Far too many riders – adults and children – have falls and suffer head injuries which could have been avoided if they had been wearing correct headgear.

Scientists who work for hat manufacturers have spent years undertaking research in an effort to make riding safer for people, and it is ridiculous for anyone to think they are right to ride without a proper hat – one that is the right size and fits correctly.

Do not rely on the riding school you attend to loan you a hat; no matter how well meaning the proprietors may be, it has not been bought for you and the chances are it will not fit your head as it should. If the hat does not fit absolutely correctly and you fall at an awkward angle or hit the ground hard, it will come off your head and immediately expose you to danger. But if it fits, and has a safety harness attached to it, your head will be protected, even from a horse's kicks. Just think what would happen if there was only your hair between your skull and a horse's shoes.

Never imagine that accidents only happen to others and not to you. Everyone is at risk when they ride, even experts, as is clearly demonstrated by the fact that all those connected with the racing world have to wear the designated headwear when riding, exercising or competing in races. The Jockey Club has made it a rule, and it is a good one. Jockeys are some of the toughest people in sport and, of course, they take more risks than the average rider, particularly when teaching young horses to jump at speed, and competing in

Make sure the hat fits

races where they might be hampered and come down or fall because their mounts make mistakes. But no matter how tough they are, they cannot avoid head injuries unless they are protected.

I mention this to highlight the fact that nobody, no matter how good or strong, is immune to injury and everyone should take the right precautions. Think safety and you will be safe.

When buying a hat, you can choose between a jockey-type skull cap (BSI number BS4472), which is the safest of all, or a velvet covered cap (6473). Whichever you decide on, there are several important points to note and no short cuts must be taken. Always look for the British Kite Mark and label – that is essential, because it means the cap has been tried and tested, and undergone vigorous safety checks to pass the standard. If the hat does not bear the distinctive Kite Mark, it is not up to the BSI standard.

Measure the circumference of your head to obtain the required size, making sure that someone helps you so that you know the exact metric measurement. Then choose the colour you want, if you are buying a velvet cap, fit it on to your head and make sure that it is comfortable and does not tilt to one side or the other. If it does, it is the wrong size and you must start again. Do not rush this particular exercise, even if it means trying on several hats.

When you have found one that fits properly, fasten the chin harness securely and make sure that you know how to fasten and unfasten it. Try it out several times and, if you are still not sure, ask the salesperson to explain in detail how it all works. It may take time but it is worth it.

If you have a rounded, or long, oval-shaped head, you may find that you need cork or foam adjusters under the head pad to give the hat a better and more comfortable fit. But be advised by the retailer and if you don't understand how it works, ask him to tell you. All hats, even velvet caps, should be fitted with a safety harness – an elastic chin strap is not safe enough because it can snap if you have a fall or bang your head on something. The latest design of hats have a safety harness attached.

A velvet cap must also have a flexible, not a rigid, peak. The reason for this is that if you do have a fall and land on your head, the peak will bend and the shock will be absorbed by the outer shell of the hat, which is specifically designed for this purpose. If it had a rigid peak, that would take the full force of the blow and could break, possibly coming downwards on to your face. There have been cases where a person's nose has been broken because of this.

Once you have bought a riding hat, make sure that you maintain it properly. Remember, it should never be dry cleaned – just brushed when dry – otherwise you could ruin it.

Some people have expressed concern about the use of a safety harness, fearing that the hat might stay firmly in place even when you did not want it to. For instance, if you were cantering and caught your head on the branch of a tree, you might either damage your neck, or even be strangled. Well, your fears can be dispelled because the harness has a breaking strain and long before it could do you serious damage it would snap open, releasing itself and you.

A lot of thought and effort have gone into everything connected with the making of hats, and the manufacturers will already have thought of any objections you might have to raise. It does them no good at all to produce inferior goods because the public will ultimately reject them. Over the years they have spent small fortunes on renewing machinery to improve riding hats so that they are safer. So do not be tempted to buy inferior imported goods which undercut the market.

Although riding hats have been designed to withstand knocks and pressure, the hat might be grazed, or even dented as a result of a fall, depending on the amount of force it has taken. A hefty wallop on the head can also cause damage to the hat in the form of stress, and so the best policy, if your hat does take a severe bashing, is to replace it with a new one – just to be safe. It is expensive, but your life could depend on it. Changing a damaged hat is much better than having another fall and being carted off to hospital with a head injury. It is not worth the risk for the sake of a few pounds. Do not penny-pinch where safety is concerned, particularly on the purchase of a new hat, because thinking ahead can save you a lot of heartache later on.

It is really astonishing how many people take chances by riding without a proper hat – they include Her Majesty the Queen and Her Royal Highness Princess Anne, a former European three-day event champion and Olympic rider. On too many occasions there have been pictures published of them riding at Sandringham, or Windsor, in headscarves or soft hats. When American President

Ronald Reagan visited the Queen and rode with her, he did not wear a proper riding hat either.

They are, of course, allowed to wear what they want but, in my opinion, it does not set a good example to young people who may follow their lead and, for their own sakes, I dearly hope they never fall off and hit their heads. The protection a headscarf affords is very slight indeed.

There is a case, too, for making showjumpers wear safety harnesses on their hats because, apart from obvious reasons, they are watched by millions of people on television when they compete at major international shows and it would set their fans a good example.

One man who does know the value of a harness on his hat is Lionel Dunning who, in the seventies, had a crashing fall from one of his horses and suffered a head injury. This courageous man did eventually recover, after a long spell on the sidelines, but now you will never see him competing without that valuable harness holding his riding hat firmly in place.

Others in his profession know what he went through and yet they still do not follow his lead. Eventers wear skull caps with a harness, as do jockeys, so why not showjumpers? It is one area where the powers that be should take action and, like the Jockey Club, bring in a rule that makes it compulsory for showjumpers to wear the correct and safest headgear. In America junior showjumpers must all wear hard hats with a harness. It is a thoroughly sensible rule. Many people do not like to be told what to do and like to keep well away from legislation but in some cases there is a definite need for the authorities to take action.

While talking about keeping the head safe, I should add that those of you who have to wear glasses must also protect your eyes. You are particularly at risk because, if you fall off, the lenses of the spectacles could shatter and damage your eyes, or the frames might break and either stick in your face or, even worse, pierce your eyes. Certainly you can take steps to help keep the glasses on, like using elastic, or tape, to fix them to your head, but accidents can still happen and it would be dreadful if you damaged your eyes.

However, there are spectacles, easily obtainable, which are made of plastic - not only the frames, but the actual lenses as well - which do not break or splinter. Which means that if and when you do fall, or the horse hits you in the face with his head, you will not suffer from glass splinters, or spectacle frame injuries.

You can, of course, use contact lenses which are the safest of all, particularly the modern, soft type. However, some people either do not like putting them in their eyes, or find them irritating. It all comes down to personal preference and it is up to the individual to work out what is best for him or her. But, if you do have to ride in glasses, it is wise to take every precaution to keep yourself safe. So make the time to visit your local optician, explain the situation, and he will advise what will be best for you.

Apart from the safety angle, it can also prove to be very expensive if you break your glasses. And it means that every time the frames or the lenses break or crack, you have to spend a lot of time getting them replaced. So try and avoid the pitfalls and get the correct pair of glasses to start with. You will save yourself a lot of problems.

4
Tethering and leading

To make your horse or pony safe and to keep your peace of mind, you must tether him properly when you want to leave him unattended for even the briefest moment. Just throwing the reins over a post, or looping them round a fence, is highly dangerous and you must not do it. They are lazy ways and can lead to your horse running loose and being hurt; they could also mean a broken or damaged bridle and can cause havoc in the stable yard, or field.

Always tether a horse or pony properly. That means using a head-collar or halter which, if necessary, you can put over his bridle. The headcollar is usually made of leather or webbing, with a hemp or nylon rope, and that rope is attached to a loop of string tied to the fence or the ring in the stable wall. When you tie the rope to the string, use a safety knot, which allows you to release the horse quickly should you need to do so. To tie the knot, the headcollar rope end is slipped through the string loop, formed into a half bow and the end attached to the headcollar is pulled tight. This forms a quick release knot – if you pull the loose end, the animal is immediately freed.

If you did not use this particular knot and the horse panicked and ran backwards, he might pull down the fence he is attached to, or break the headcollar he is wearing. Either way it leads to problems which can be avoided if you do things correctly in the first place.

Many horses and ponies are fine when they are tethered and would not dream of pulling back, or causing a fuss in any way. But there are some who hate to be tied and they are the ones likely to hurt themselves. If, however, you have tied him correctly, a swift sharp

His head might be sensitive

tug on the end of the rope will realease him and give you time to settle him down again and give him confidence.

Some people object to the use of a headcollar over a bridle, but it does no harm and can prove very convenient if you are in a hurry, and do not have time to take the bridle off and replace it with a headcollar. Just make sure that you do not fit the headcollar too tightly so that the bit hurts his mouth, or the cheekpieces of the bridle dig into him.

When you are not using the headcollar put it in the tack room. Too often I see headcollars and other tack strewn all over the place, hanging from stable doors, or lying about on the yard getting dirty. It does not take long to return the headcollar to the safety of the tack room. It is tidier to do so and will save you losing it.

When you have tethered your mount do not leave him alone for too long because he will become bored and start to do silly things like chewing the fence, or stamping with impatience. Have his welfare in mind and see to his needs before your own.

The worst type of stable yard is one where you see row upon row of horses and ponies tethered to rails or fences, with nothing to occupy their minds until someone comes along and takes them out on a ride. Horses are not machines and should not be treated like bicycles, which you can put on one side until you want to ride again. When you have finished with your mount for the day, make sure that he is comfortable, groom him, even if that means just tidying him up with a body brush, and then, if he lives out, turn him into his field.

If you want to feed your pony while he is tethered, make sure that the headcollar rope is long enough for him to be able to reach the bin in which you have put the food. There is no point securing him properly so that he cannot pull away if he cannot eat his food because the rope is tied too short. Also, be certain that the bin you use for the feed is sturdy and cannot tip over on to his legs. Even if it does not hit and hurt his legs, the noise of a feed bin falling over can have a dreadful effect on some horses and they will pull back in fright.

It is also wise to make certain that your horse is far enough away from any other horse or pony tethered nearby, because some greedy mounts, once they have finished their own food, will attempt to eat that belonging to another horse. It is up to you to be sure that such a horse cannot reach food that does not belong to him.

Another way of tethering a horse with a headcollar, and one I do not like, is to attach a ball of wood, or a log, to the end of the rope. Before the ball is fixed, the rope is run through the metal holder on the stable wall and the ball is put on afterwards and held secure by a quick release knot. The idea is that the ball takes the slack out of the rope and the animal cannot then get a leg caught over it. It is not cruel in any way, but I think that if the horse became frightened and ran backwards, the ball on the end of the rope would be forced up into the ring, making an unearthly racket which would scare the horse even more.

The best way to keep a horse or pony happy is for him to be interested in what is happening around him; yet, at the same time, he should have the security of peace and quiet. When horses have been working hard, they need to rest and the least noise can sometimes upset them. That is another reason why I do not advocate the use of the 'ball on the end of the rope' method.

Headcollars must always fit correctly; the headband should lay flat behind the horse's ears, with the side pieces hanging straight down behind the cheekbones. Once you have put the headcollar on, you should be able to put two fingers between the nose band and the animal's nose. If the band is too tight it will hurt him and restrict his breathing.

A rope halter must also fit correctly and it is important to knot the lead rope at the side of the noseband to prevent undue tightening by the slip knot. If this sort of equipment is used to the best advantage and put on properly, you and your mount will be a lot safer.

Some horses hate having anything put on their heads, and the moment someone tries to put on a headcollar they throw their heads into the air and either run backwards, or just hold their heads so high that you cannot get anywhere near them. There are several reasons for this behaviour; one is that they might, at some time, have been hit about the face with a headcollar and are terrified of it; another, is that they might easily have a sensitive spot on the part where the headcollar rests.

The only way to deal with this is with patience and understanding although, at times, you will most certainly feel like tearing your hair out in frustration, particularly if you are in a hurry and your mount starts backing off when you want to put the headcollar on him. Whatever else you do, do not lose your temper because that will only serve to make matters worse. Spend some time trying to reassure him. Talk to him, put your right arm over his neck slowly, and gradually work your way up to where the headcollar goes. At this stage you are merely trying to gain his confidence and the headcollar should be nowhere in sight. It is just a question of making him feel at ease. The object of the exercise is to get him used to having something touching the top of his neck and ears and, eventually, he will accept that you are not trying to hurt him. But I must warn you it can take a lot of time, particularly if he is frightened. When you think that he is ready to accept the headcollar without any fuss, try and put it on him. But if he does run back, or puts his head in the air out of reach, do not wave the headcollar at him. Remain calm and keep on trying.

Then there are horses who, once you turn them out, just do not want to be caught. This can be infuriating because it means you can sometimes spend upwards of half an hour walking around a field. Some horses will even allow you to walk right up to them and then, at the last moment, turn and gallop off to the other end of the paddock. It sounds fun but it certainly is not if you do not have the time to waste.

This is one occasion when I would not object to the animal being turned out with a headcollar on, because then at least you have something to hold on to when he attempts to gallop off out of reach. Normally I would not advocate leaving a headcollar on a horse at grass because it might get caught up on something and he could hurt himself. But, with a horse who just refuses to be caught, you must try and make things easier for yourself.

If you do turn your mount out with a headcollar on, always check and make sure that there are not any twigs or burrs lodged under the headpiece when you bring him in out of the field. It only takes a few seconds to check and could save him making his head sore.

The best thing to do with a horse who runs off is to try and encourage him to look forward to you stepping into his field. Many horses recognize their owner's voice from a long way off. The good ones come the moment you call. If, however, yours is somewhat wayward, the best thing to do is offer him a titbit – a lump of sugar or something else you happen to know he likes. It is bribery, but it sometimes works and you might find that, instead of tearing off, he will actually get used to you giving him a reward for being good.

Having dealt with headcollars, it is most important for you to know how to lead a horse or pony in hand properly. You might think it is just a question of grabbing the lead rein and pulling your mount where you want him to go. But there is a lot more to it than that, and to be safe you must know what you are doing. Always remember that a horse can be just as dangerous when you are leading him, as he can when you are actually on his back. Certainly when you are leading you cannot fall off, but you can be dragged and that can end disastrously.

To bring a horse or pony out of his stable you must think about what you are doing and never, ever, allow him to rush through the doorway as though he were being chased by a thousand demons. You must take things calmly and gently and instil confidence into him at all times. Some stables have very small openings for their doorways, although they should not have, and if this is the case your mount, if you are not careful, could bash into the door with his hip and either bruise or cut himself. One answer is to turn him around and go through it backwards. It may be somewhat unorthodox but it is far better to do that than risk him hurting himself because he is either frightened or just plain silly.

When you are in the stable area it is quite all right to lead your mount in a halter, or a headcollar, if he is quiet and sensible, but when you go on lanes or roads you must put a bridle on him. (It is illegal not to.) You do this because you then have more control over him and he has less chance of getting away and causing untold damage to himself and anyone else in the near vicinity.

To lead a horse, place your right hand palm round the rope or reins about eight or ten inches from the bridle or the headcollar. Never hold the actual headcollar itself or the bridle right up near the animal's head, because many horses hate this and you will cause them to fight you, or pull back. And when you are leading a horse or pony this is the last thing you want to happen.

The slack of the rope or the reins is then held in the left hand because (a) this gives you more control and (b) it takes up the slack and prevents it flying about all over the place. Apart from the safety

angle, it also looks neat and tidy and that is how it should be at all
times.

In order to get your horse or pony to do exactly what you want
him to do at any given time, you must train him to a certain extent,
even when you want simply to lead him in hand. There are only one
or two minor commands to remember and once he has learnt what
you want, life becomes so much easier and safer for both of you. For
example, when you have put the bridle or headcollar on him and are
about to walk him from a standstill to another part of the stable yard
or field, give him a pat on the neck and say 'walk on'.

The same method can be used for turning him to the right or to
the left by merely saying 'now left' or 'now right'. Do not worry
about making yourself look or sound silly because gaining and keeping your mount's confidence is far more important than what you
feel or look like. Given the commands often enough your horse or
pony will become accustomed to them, and you will be surprised
how good it makes you feel when he does what you ask. It will also
stop you pulling or yanking him about.

One very important point to keep in mind when leading in hand is
never to turn your horse towards you, always turn him away from
your body. This means that when you are turning left, you should
change hands and go to his offside (right) and turn him the way you
want him to go to the left. The reason for this is that if you turned the
animal in towards you, and he became excited, he would tread all
over your feet. And anyone who has ever had a horse stand on them
will know exactly how painful it is and that, if you are unlucky, you
could end up with broken toes or, at the least, a very badly bruised
foot.

And even if you were lucky enough to escape injury, it could possibly lead to you losing your temper and pulling down hard on the
bridle or headcollar and frightening him. That is all it takes for a
horse to lose all confidence in you, and the next time you attempted
to put him on a lead rein and walk him out, you might be faced with
a certain amount of difficulty.

Horses and ponies are a lot stronger than you and that is one of the
reasons you must never lead a horse with the rope or the reins
wrapped around your hands or wrists. You may think that you have
enough sense not to do this but, in an unguarded moment, or when

you think the reins or rope might be slipping out of your hands, you might just do something like that. Well, do not, as it is highly dangerous.

There have been reported cases where children have been leading ponies and they have wound the rope around their hands and then the animals have become excited, or frightened, and have dashed off, pulling the unfortunate youngsters behind them. In one case, at least, the child could not free himself and was pulled over and dragged for more than a hundred yards along a stony lane. As he was being pulled along, the hind legs of the pony he was leading kept dashing against his head; he was taken to hospital with very serious injuries, from which he did not recover.

I tell you this dreadful thing, not to frighten or upset you, but to bring home fully the message that you must never, under any circumstances, wrap the reins or the lead rope around your hands. Certainly some horses will try and get loose and many will play you up terribly. But just hold the reins or the rope as I have described and no harm will come to you or your mount.

You must not only think of yourself at a time when your horse or pony is being silly and pulling – you should also be aware of the havoc which would be caused if he were to get loose and dash off up the road. If that happened he would be in danger and so would anyone else who was around, at the time. Unfortunately, when a horse is loose, he does tend to panic because it is a completely strange situation he finds himself in, and although he certainly does not want to hurt people, all too often he does.

He is quite likely to leap away and run into main highways without a second thought, and motorists, many of whom know nothing about horses and ponies anyway, might run into him, causing fearful damage. Some drivers do know about animals and, if they see a loose one careering towards them, will stop and cut out some of the danger. But others, like the animal in full flight, will panic and keep going, when anything can happen.

But at the end of the day, because the horse or pony is in your charge, the responsibility rests with you. So try, whatever else you do, to hold on to him. The main reason is that you do not want him hurting anyone else, or himself and you certainly do not want someone suing you for damages. All of this can be avoided if you hold on to the reins and try and train your horse to walk sensibly and quietly when making your way from one place to another.

Having told you how to come out of a stable, if your horse has a tendency to rush through doorways you must also learn how to cope when leading him back into his stable. If he rushes out, the odds are that he will want to rush back in again. This tends to be a difficult situation and you must be very careful how you handle it, because you could end up being trodden on or knocked over. Go in before your mount but do not walk directly in front of him. Stand to one side, about an arm's length in front of his forelegs, hold firmly on to the bridle and keep talking to him. If you feel him getting stronger and stronger, try and keep him steady until the doorway has been negotiated, and try not to let him fling his head up into the air because he might strike it on the doorway. If this happens, he could develop poll evil, which is an abscess on the head caused by a blow. It can be cured, but the horse becomes extremely sensitive around the poll and the ears and it could be some time before he will allow you to touch him there.

One of the favourite tricks of youngsters when they have a pony is to walk him around the stable yard on a lead rein, and then toss the rein over the animal's neck and let him walk around unescorted. It is a ridiculous thing to do because any sudden movement could frighten him, and he will immediately be at risk if he dashes away from the safety of the stable area. It is not clever, so never do it. You might own the calmest horse or pony in the stable and one who never ever does anything wrong. But remember, there is always a first time for everything.

I have even seen young riders saddle up and then allow their mounts to wander off without supervision to the water trough to get a drink before they go on their ride. Never do this. Apart from the dangers involved, he could also step on the hanging reins of the bridle and break them. And, if he did that, he could also hurt his mouth and you could have a double disaster on your hands.

5

A stitch in time

One of the most dangerous things you can do is to ride when your tack is defective. Stirrup leathers can break, bridles and girths can fray and weaken, causing you to fall off your mount and be hurt.

The way to be safe in the saddle is to make regular checks of your equipment and if you think the stitching is wearing, or the leather is not up to par, take it to the saddler and ask him to check it over. It does not cost a lot of money to have stitching strengthened, just your time, and that could save you an awful lot in the long run. If the tack is well looked after in the first place, you will not have any problems.

If you are just about to buy a saddle and bridle, do not go for the cheapest you can find. You might think at the time that they are bargains, but there is a lot more to it than that. You must be safe. As far as the saddle is concerned, it must be one that fits you and your pony correctly, and the same applies to the bridle. Once you have established the correct size, shop around for the best value. And that does not mean the cheapest.

There is on the market today a lot of inferior tack which has been imported from far flung places in the world where labour is much cheaper than here in European countries. Because the labour costs are lower in those countries, the tack can be churned out at ridiculously low prices. But, there is usually a catch to it all, in some cases because the leather used is inferior and does not last as long as the equipment made in Britain. British tack is always up to a certain standard. Manufacturers do not supply goods that fall apart in a few months or even a few years.

Some imported tack, however, leaves a lot to be desired and I would advise you not to buy a saddle or bridle which is imported from half-way around the world, yet only costs half the price of British-made tack. Save up and pay for the best: it will be much cheaper for you in the long run. Remember, you only get what you pay for.

When buying your tack, take an experienced horseperson with you to guide you through the pitfalls. And once bought, it must be maintained properly. That is the key to it all; and you will be safe into the bargain.

You should clean your tack after every use and that means that you wash off any mud with tepid water and then soap it to keep it supple. Then, every four or five days I suggest that you completely dismantle the bridle and saddle, check to make sure that all the stitching is sound and thoroughly clean the leather. The fact is that if you do not work out a sensible system for these jobs the leather could become dry and crack. Cleaning does not take very long and once you have established a sensible routine everything will come that much easier to you.

The first thing to do is to make sure that you have all that you require for the job, and that involves a little thought, too, because there is no use at all being very keen and wanting to clean your tack if, when you start, you have not the materials with which to do it. Make sure that you have a bucket, sponge, stable rubbers, a tin of saddle soap, and a hard brush to knock off any mud which may be clinging to the saddle and bridle. You will also need something to poke out any muck that has collected in the holes of the stirrup leathers and the bridle – a dead matchstick or small nail will do – and a duster to polish up the bit on the bridle.

If you cannot work on a table, then make sure you have a sheet available to put on the tack room floor, or the floor of your garage, so that any dust or dirt that may be around does not stick to the leather once you have applied the saddle soap. It can be infuriating to work for an hour and then discover bits of hair sticking to the leather.

When you have everything at hand set it out so that it is within easy reach. Try to plan the cleaning operation well, because fiddling about looking for equipment wastes time. Make a mental note of where everything is and you will not have any problems.

Never soak leather in water

Having stripped the bridle, make sure that you place it on the cloth so that you know how to put it back together again. For example, put the headpiece of the bridle at the top, the browband just underneath that, with the cheek pieces and reins on either side. Then dip your sponge in tepid water, wring it out well and clean one item at a time, making sure that you do the job well, washing away any mud or sweat from the leather. When you have done this, replace the item and go on to the next part of the bridle. Take your time and think about what you are doing; never rush the tack cleaning job because if you do you will miss parts of the leather and it will have all been a waste of time.

When you have washed off the mud and sweat from the bridle, and I mean every section of it, either allow it to dry by itself or encourage it to do so by rubbing it with a clean cloth. By this time the leather will be fairly parched and have a rough feel about it and this is the time to apply the saddle soap to every part of the bridle. Take the browband first and gently rub the sponge into the tin or bar of soap so that you have a thin film of it covering the outer edge of the sponge. Then pick up the browband and rub the sponge over it, giving the soap time to penetrate the leather.

Remember that it is the rough underside of the leather that is best able to absorb the saddle soap, so do not just apply it to the smooth upper surface. You might find at this stage that your fingers are becoming rather sticky and you may feel you are doing more harm than good to the leather. Well, wipe that thought right out of your mind because you are, in fact, doing it a power of good, even if you do feel like leaving at once and washing the saddle soap off your hands. What you must realize is that when you are doing cleaning jobs on, or for, horses you will get yourself dirty. You can always have a good wash once the exercise is over, so do not worry about it but get on with the work.

I have even known some mothers tell their daughters that it is a job they should not be doing because they consider that the water and saddle soap ruin their hands. That is absolute rubbish and, although some mothers might think you ought to be doing something more ladylike, in this modern day and age, girls expect, and the majority probably want, to get stuck into the chores just like the boys. As far as ruining your hands is concerned, you can always apply some hand cream later on, so that argument does not hold good.

When you have cleaned the browband, put it back in its place on the sheet and concentrate on the main body of the bridle. The same procedure is adopted for cleaning this, although if you have rubber on the ends of the reins, do not put saddle soap on them. Just wash the rubber and dry it. The reason for this is that if you put soap on the rubber, it would not soak in, and when you went riding the reins would slip through your hands.

After cleaning the main part of the bridle, replace it on the sheet and start to work on the noseband. As you clean each part check that the stitching is in good order. Normally a quick glance at an assembled bridle will not tell you very much, so take the opportunity to have a good look now.

When you have finished working on the leather start on the actual bit because this is just as important as the bridle itself. A worn or rough bit can cause havoc with your horse's mouth and if the one you have has seen better days, then replace it at once. If you do not, it will cut his cheeks and lips and it would be irresponsible of you to allow him to be harmed in such a manner. Apart from that, you will not be able to ride him for a while.

If the bit is all right, and there are no rough edges or it has not worn down at all, dip the metal in tepid water, wash off any gunge and then polish it with a clean cloth. As the bit goes in the horse's mouth you must not put polish on the metal. Just wash it and apply a lot of elbow grease. That will keep it clean and your horse healthy.

Many people will recommend that when you are cleaning a bridle you should hang the pieces on a peg to do it. Well, I do not agree, particularly if you are new at the job. I have known several people try to clean a bridle in this way and when they have gone to reassemble it they could not. That does not surprise me because until you have had some experience with tack most of you will not know what you are doing. So clean the bridle in the way I suggest and you will find everything that much easier.

Another point to remember when cleaning bridles is never, ever, put any of the leather into water and let it soak. That will make the leather stretch. Just wash the sweat marks off with a cloth or sponge and then dry and soap them.

Above   Always thank the driver as he slows to pass

Below   A good roller will keep the rug in place

The correct way to tie a quick release knot

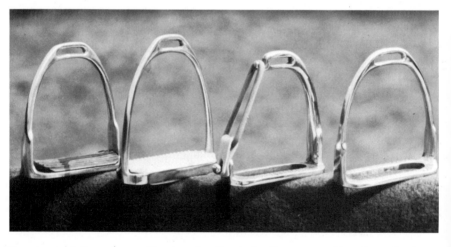

Four types of stirrup iron, rubber based, safety and ordinary types. Note the rubber band on the side of the safety iron

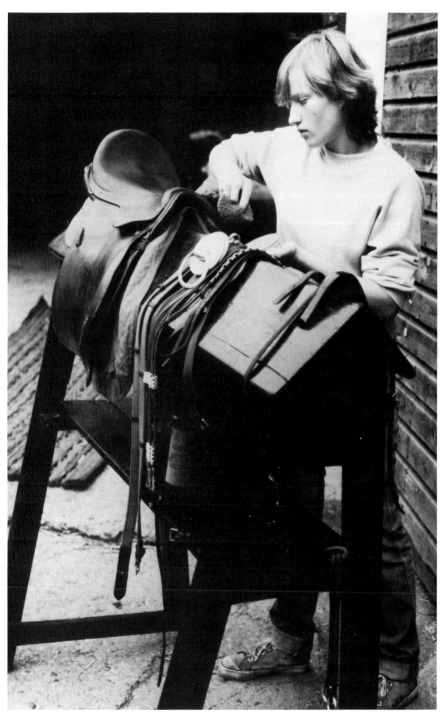

The way to preserve tack and keep it in good order is to clean it regularly. Always use a
saddle horse if you can

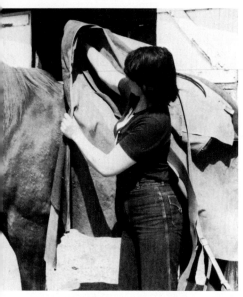

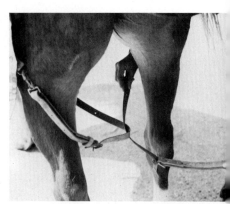

Left Make sure you place the New Zealand rug correctly on the horse's back

Below Leg straps to prevent the New Zealand rug slipping must be secured at the back as shown

A jute rug must be brushed to keep it free of foreign objects

To clean the saddle you will need the use of a saddle horse to keep it steady. If you allow the saddle to move about on its gullet, it might damage it. If you do not have the use of a saddle horse, then you will have to improvise. But keep the saddle firmly held when cleaning.

First, knock off any mud that may be clinging to the saddle; then strip the saddle by taking off the stirrup leathers and the girths, and start by sponging off the sweat and dirt marks from the under side. Hold the saddle over a bucket of tepid (never hot) water and wash the mud off so that the water will run off the saddle and not soak the lining. When this has been done, dry it with a clean cloth and then apply saddle soap. But again you must work in clean conditions otherwise you will find that specks of dust, dirt and hairs will cling to the soap.

When you have completed the under edge put the saddle on the saddle horse and work on the seat, washing and drying it and the flaps. After this apply saddle soap and rub in vigorously. You might find that the saddle flaps are fairly stiff and if they are then really get to work on them using plenty of elbow grease, and not forgetting the underside. Remember, however, not to put too much saddle soap on the seat because if you do it might mark your jodhpurs.

When you have completed the work on the saddle it is time to begin cleaning the stirrup leathers. Take the leather off the stirrup iron and rub with a wet sponge to clean off any mud or sweat. When you have done this, poke the holes where the stirrup leather pin goes with a nail or dead matchstick to unblock them. Wash off with a sponge of water, dry and then apply the saddle soap. I like leathers to be very supple because if they are stiff and hard the chances are they will eventually crack, which would be dangerous. If they are stiff it is also very difficult to change the length of leather when you are riding. Rub plenty of saddle soap into the stirrup leathers and bend them about. When they are supple you will know you have done a good job.

After you have cleaned the leathers properly, hang them over the saddle horse to allow the soap plenty of time to soak in. Then start to work on the irons. Wash any mud or muck off them, dry with a clean cloth and then apply metal polish and rub them up until they shine.

After this has been done it is time to work on the girths, not only for your safety but for the comfort of your horse or pony as well. If you allow the girths to remain stiff and dirty your mount will most certainly suffer from girth galls and they are very unpleasant. Equally, if you do not bother to keep them clean they could crack and break, which would mean you and the saddle would fall off the animal's back.

If they are made of leather, wash them thoroughly with your sponge of tepid water and make sure that all the muck and sweat is cleaned off. When this has been accomplished, and the leather rubbed dry with a cloth, put the soap on and rub in well. Also polish up the buckles until they sparkle. When finished hang up on a hook to allow the soap well and truly to soak into the leather.

If your girths are the webbing or nylon type, you must brush them and then wash them out well. But if you do this make absolutely sure that they are rinsed out thoroughly after washing. Like the leather girths, they can then be hung up to keep clean until you want to use them, or put back on to the clean saddle.

If you are very young, and your saddle is made of felt, all you have to do is brush off the mud and then run a damp sponge over the felt to clean it. But of course the normal methods of cleaning apply to the leathers and the girths.

Also, make a note to condition your leather tack with neatsfoot oil two or three times a year (preferably when it won't be used for a few days). This is applied to washed but unsoaped leather with a soft dry cloth. Rub the oil well in and leave it to soak in naturally for as long as possible.

Apart from the saddle and bridle there are also other things you have to keep clean. They include headcollar, stable rubbers and pads and numnahs (a pad which goes under the saddle). If your headcollar is made of webbing this must be brushed and then washed and the stitching checked every time you do so. The numnah must also be washed and cleaned according to the maker's instructions and allowed to air.

One important point that you must always remember when cleaning and washing leather or webbing is never to put it over a fire or hot radiator to dry. If you do, the leather will crack and that is very dangerous; it is also extremely expensive to replace. Even if the leather does not crack, the stitching will most certainly do so. You must exercise a lot of patience when cleaning tack and think about what you are doing. There are no short cuts. It is hard work and it takes time to do things properly.

To give you some idea of the importance of tack it is best to know how a saddle is made up, because once you know that you can then treat it with the respect it deserves. For example, the main part of any saddle is the tree and if this is cracked or broken, the saddle becomes useless. The tree is the main structure and runs from the pommel (the front) to the cantle (the back) and if you drop your saddle, or throw it in the corner when you have finished using it, the chances are you will either break or damage that structure. The materials used for making the tree are usually laminated beech plywood, plastic or fibre-glass. However, a spring-tree saddle has a piece of steel, which is flexible, put in it, too.

The saddle flaps are the parts on which your knees are placed, or should be, when you are riding and underneath those are the panels which are filled with felt or sometimes wool. There are half sized panels and full sized ones. Over these are the girth straps which hold the girths firmly in place when the saddle is on your horse's back. Inserted on to the girth straps is a buckle guard which can be moved up and down and is placed over the girth buckles to prevent the metal sticking into the saddle flaps and damaging them.

The metal stirrup bars are situated just under what is called the skirt of the saddle and are fixed to the tree. The stirrup leathers are placed round the bars, which take your weight when you are mounted. As I mention in the chapter on how to mount your horse, at one end of each bar there is a hinged piece which can be moved up so that it is at right angles to the main part of the bar. Its purpose is to prevent the stirrup leather from slipping off the bar but this can be extremely dangerous. If you had the so-called 'safety bars' up, and you fell off, you could be dragged, because the stirrup leather would not come away from the stirrup bar. If when you insert the leathers you leave the bar as it is, the leather will be pulled off the saddle by your weight tugging on it, and you will be freed from your horse's flaying hooves.

But remember that your leathers must be a perfect fit if they are not to slip from the bars when you are riding. That will only happen if the leathers are worn and thin, and if they are, they should be replaced at once. Do not take chances because, if you think about it, those leathers take your weight when you are mounted and must always be in prime condition.

A good saddle is worth its weight in gold and at least once a year you must make sure that the stuffing is still doing its job. If it is not, and the saddle is pressing down on the animal's spine, you must take the saddle to a saddler and ask for it to be restuffed. It is not expensive and it will help keep the saddle in good working order.

If you drop your saddle and want to test it to see if the tree is broken, just make sure that the cantle (the tip of the saddle at the very back end) is rigid; if you can move it about then the saddle is useless and will have to be replaced. With a spring tree saddle, just hold the pommel with one hand and the cantle with the other and pull towards you. If the tree is weakened it will not, as its name implies, spring back into place. If you have not the strength to test the spring tree saddle as I have suggested, put the pommel of the saddle into your stomach muscles, hold the cantle with both hands and pull slowly towards yourself. If you find that there is a lot of resistance do not worry because that means the tree is certainly not broken or weak.

Apart from the saddle tree you must also check that the front arch of the saddle is okay and not worn, and does not have bits of leather hanging from it. The arch is the part which fits over the horse's withers and is the area from which the gullet of the saddle starts. If the surface of the arch is broken, it will press down on the animal's withers and make him very sore. This type of injury takes a long time to heal and when it happens your horse cannot be ridden. If you are in any doubt about the structure of the arch, take it along to a saddler and ask him to have a look at it for you.

Even if a saddle fits well, I have always been a firm believer in using a saddle pad, which looks something like a folded tea-towel, and takes a lot of pressure off the horse's withers. I would always use one that has been well washed and so has lost a lot of its new crispness and is soft and very pliable. In this condition it most certainly will not hurt the animal's skin in any way.

The whole secret of keeping your saddle and bridle in good order is to look after them properly, and I do not mean just keeping them clean. Even the way you carry a saddle is important: as mentioned earlier, to do this you should either put the arch of it in the crease of your elbow with your arm along the gullet, or hold the pommel with your left hand and have the underside of the saddle resting up against your body. Either way is correct, and it is just a matter of what is comfortable for you. The reason for carrying the saddle in this manner is that it is easy and it helps protect the leather which, if you were to drag it along, or hold the saddle by the leathers, could easily be damaged.

When you have finished with the saddle it should be placed on the saddle rack in the tack room with the girths and the leathers stripped from it. They should be hung on their respective pegs until the next time they are used. If you need to put the saddle down before reaching the tack room, there are two ways of doing this. Fold the girth and either place the pommel of the saddle on it so that the saddle is, as it were, standing on its head, or put the folded girth under the pommel and up over the cantle so that the saddle can rest against a wall without scratching the leather. Some people lay the saddle down flat, with the flaps sticking out, but I do not like this method because somebody might fall over it, or stand on the arch and damage it in some way. It is amazing how clumsy some people can be and it is not worth taking chances.

So remember to keep your tack like new, look after it and every day check that the stitching is firm and not worn. Never take chances and if anything looks wrong with the saddle or bridle, get someone to give you a second opinion. It is far better to have stitching mended and leather made secure than to try and mend a broken arm or leg. Because, believe me, that is what can happen if your tack is faulty. The answer is to be alert, work hard and be safe.

6

How to mount your horse

Preparing to mount is as important as actually doing so, because if you try to rush the procedure you might frighten the horse and spend a lot of time trying to calm him. The secret of success when riding is to take your time and do things right. When you approach the horse you should talk to him in a gentle, welcoming voice to let him know that you are a friend and do not intend him any harm.

If you were to dash around and fling yourself at him, the chances are you would end up on the ground, with a loose horse running about the stable yard. Keep calm, transmit confidence and nothing will go wrong.

Keep your mind free of everything except your mount. When you first walk up to him make a fuss of him, give him a pat on the neck and tell him what a clever boy he is; everyone likes praise, and animals are no exception. All it takes on your part is a small amount of consideration.

The first thing you should do before mounting is to check the girths. If you find they are slack, tighten them up a hole or two until the saddle feels firm and in place. Try to mount with a loose girth and you will slide under the horse's tummy. When the saddle check has been completed, give his bridle a look over and make sure it, too, is correctly fitted.

Run the stirrup irons down the leathers, making sure they are the right length for you. You can work out roughly what length you need by putting your closed hand on the stirrup bar under the flap, and adjusting the leather until the stirrup iron rests under your armpit.

Failure to adjust your leathers can lead to all sorts of complications, particularly if the saddle has been used by someone else with much shorter, or longer, legs. If you do not check the length of the leathers before climbing into the saddle, and they happen to be much too short, you might have to do a balancing act while you adjust them. And if the pony you are riding is a restive type, it can be a very uncomfortable business.

Some people advocate mounting from either the nearside or the offside, but I do not agree. In the old cavalry days when they had to mount quickly, it might have been all right to get on from the right but that does not apply now and the side from which to mount is the left. Some experts say that it does not matter; my answer is that it does, because one of the ways to successful riding is to have a correct procedure for doing everything. Mounting from the right side is unorthodox, and should only be done in exceptional cases – for example, if you are handicapped and it is easier for you.

When you have made all the necessary tack checks it is time to mount. Hold the reins in your left hand and turn your back to the horse's head. Hold the offside rein slightly shorter than the nearside one, so that if the animal tries to nip or bite, his head is controlled to a certain extent by the rein. But do not hold the reins too short or too tight; there must be just enough contact with his mouth to retain control.

Take the stirrup iron in your right hand and twist it so that you can place your left foot into it with your toes pointing down. If you push your foot into the iron any old way, your boot might stick into the horse's tummy and hurt him, or make him fidget at the very time you want him to remain still. Having put your left foot into the iron correctly, grip the front of the saddle with your right hand, push up from the ground with your right leg, turn and spring quickly and quietly into the saddle. Do not hang on to the back of the saddle when mounting as this can twist it out of shape.

If you have a horse who is rather naughty and will not stand still, ask someone at the stables to hold his head for you while you mount. That way you will have complete control and will be able to mount with the minimum of fuss. When you are first starting out do not try to be too clever or attempt things that might be beyond you. Seek and accept help when you think it necessary and if you believe

Retain contact with his mouth

someone should hold the animal's head, ask them to do so. There is nothing worse than to make a spectacle of yourself with horses, or be terrified or unsure of the horse you are riding. It is always better to ask for help than to suffer in silence and be uncomfortable. Everyone has to start somewhere and there is certainly no harm in seeking help or advice. In fact, where horses are concerned, never think you know it all or be too proud to ask for assistance.

It can also be beneficial to have someone give you a leg-up into the saddle - particularly if you are on the short side and are riding a big horse. This simply means that you stand facing the saddle, holding the reins with your left hand, while the helper holds your left leg below the knee and slightly above the ankle. As you spring up, your helper gives you the added impulsion you need to reach the saddle.

If there is nobody at the stables to help you, you can always use a mounting block, which is rather a genteel way of doing things. The block is usually made of wood or stone, and you position your horse or pony alongside, on the right side of the block. Then, again holding the reins in the left hand, you step up on the block, place your foot in the nearside stirrup iron and swing into the saddle. It is quick, easy and requires little effort on the part of the rider.

When mounting there is another golden rule you must remember and that is never to bump down heavily into the saddle. That sort of movement can frighten a horse. The thing to do is to practise getting on and off until you know how it should be done properly.

There is one other way to mount, but I would advise this method only for the person who has had a lot of riding experience. This is to vault into the saddle. To accomplish this you stand on the nearside of your horse, with the reins in your left hand. Place your left hand on the horse's withers and your right hand on the saddle, and then spring up so that the centre of your tummy is resting over the centre of the saddle; once in that position you swivel your right leg over and at the same time turn your head and upper body toward the horse's head and sit upright.

This is a very athletic way of doing things and you must be absolutely sure you can manage it with the minimum of fuss, otherwise you could find yourself going round in ever decreasing circles, lying across the top of the saddle, half on and half off. Jockeys favour this way of mounting because they are extremely fit and it is quick and easy for them. They also know that a racehorse does not stand still for long and that they have to be in control as quickly as possible. They are fit because they have to be. But your muscles will not be as hard or your timing as accurate as theirs, so it is best to stick to the conventional way of mounting.

But you can learn something from jockeys. When young racing hopefuls set out they have to start from the beginning just as you do; many of them are not allowed anywhere near a racehorse until they have been taught to sit on a pony, or a hack, kept in the racing stable for that specific purpose. You can imagine what would happen if a young boy or girl, just starting out in racing, was put straight away onto a fit Thoroughbred. The result, in most cases, would be disastrous. They, too, have to learn the hard way and start at the bottom.

The first thing they learn is how to mount and sit correctly in the saddle, and it can sometimes be a painful experience. In my youth I spent the first few weeks in a racing stable learning to ride a wooden horse or a large barrel, in an attempt to strengthen leg muscles which, by the end of my getting-fit period, were almost screaming for mercy.

But the lesson was important because to ride you must be fit. It is never just a question of balance. The muscles of your thighs and calves must be strong, and the only way to get them used to riding is to ride. If you cannot afford the money, or the time, to go riding regularly, practise on the arm of a chair, or turn a dining room chair the reverse way and sit on that, gripping the sides with your legs. You will be amazed how that helps get you fit.

Once mounted on a horse or pony, sit in the saddle and relax – do not tense up, or fidget. Then make sure your stirrup leathers are the right length and equal in length either side. Riding with uneven stirrups causes you to be unbalanced. If they do not feel level, alter them by lifting your leg forward and taking hold of the tongue of the leather with your hand. Once you have a firm grip, pull the tongue up to release the buckle pin, at the same time pressing down with your foot into the stirrup iron. When the pin is free you can select any hole in the leather, up, or down, to make sure your leg is level with the other one.

When you have made sure that your stirrups are as they should be, your next job is to hold the reins correctly. You must not tug on them, or hold them as you would a Christmas cracker. More horses' and ponies' mouths have been ruined by people with 'bad' hands than I care to remember. Your fingers should be able to feel the weight of the horse's mouth and head and your hands should give with their movements.

Never panic and start pulling your horse's mouth about if he is naughty. Just take things quietly and calmly and keep your hands down on his neck. The worst thing you can do is to shout at him and wave your arms and the reins about as though you had fallen in the water and were trying unsuccessfully to swim. Sit, suffer and remain in control of the situation, with your hands feeling and correcting the horse's movements as you see fit. Remember, the horse is a herd animal and is used to being led. You must be the leader and show him what you want of him. But do it quietly and efficiently, using your hands in the gentlest way.

A horse hates being jagged in the mouth and also dislikes walking along with his head shoved in his chest for any length of time. Remember, you need only light contact with his mouth, not a vice-like grip, which might damage the sides of his mouth and ruin the skin of your hands at the same time. On some occasions you might find that the horse or pony you are riding has a dreadful habit of pulling the reins out of your hands and shaking his head about. Do not reprimand him before finding out why he is doing it.

Make sure that the bit fits correctly and that he has not managed to get his tongue over the top of it. If all is well there, and he continues to throw his head down, bridge the reins over the top of his neck just in front of the saddle. That way you will not pull him about too much in anger, or frustration, and when he tries to put his head down again he will be pulling against his own neck and will soon give up. To bridge the reins you simply cross one rein over the other, so that the cross section forms a bridge.

To hold your reins in the correct way, the leather should run between the little finger of either hand and the finger next to it, with the thumbs holding the reins firmly. The front of your hand should be facing forward and your wrists should be straight, not bent in, or out. It is important to ride with your reins at the right length. If they are too short, you will feel unbalanced and awkward, and if they are too long, you will lose a certain amount of control. There is a happy medium and it is up to you to find out what suits you and your mount. And remember never to ride with your elbows sticking out and flapping around. Keep them tucked in to your sides. The secret of good, enjoyable riding is to feel right and that means keeping your elbows in and your wrists straight. Your body should be like one unit, not as if it is about to fall into a thousand pieces.

When tightening the girths or stirrup leathers you will need to know how to hold the reins in one hand, and you should learn to do this in the simplest and most effective way possible. When you need to adjust anything on your left hand side, hold the reins in your right hand, with the middle three fingers bridging both reins and keep that hand down on the horse's neck. Reverse the procedure when tackling anything on the offside.

Although many people consider that a young rider should not be allowed to carry a whip, I don't agree. The only time a whip is dangerous is when the person holding it misuses it. But it is most certainly a good aid, and youngsters should get used to carrying one. Sometimes your mount might need a slight reprimand because he is being naughty, and a tap from a whip will often straighten him out, and stop him being silly.

The whip can be carried in either hand and is placed against the palm of the hand and held in place with the thumb. The butt should point towards the horse's head. The biggest danger about a whip is you: you must learn to control yourself and not use it just when you feel like it. *Never* slap a horse because you have lost your temper. If a whip is used incorrectly it can be very painful.

When you do really need to reprimand a horse or pony, one sharp slap on the bottom is usually enough to make him realize that what he has done is wrong. Never hit him under the tummy, or on the head, because that can hurt terribly. The skin under his body is much thinner than that on his rear and is not protected by hardened muscle. So hitting him there would be very unfair. Carry a whip, by all means, but be responsible for all your actions and do not lose your temper.

When you are actually mounted, look and feel good. If you sit in the saddle like a sack of sawdust, or a bag of potatoes there is no real point in it at all. Even if it takes time, work at it, make yourself do things properly and take pride in what you are doing. Sit as though you own the world, but make sure you sit in the middle of the saddle with your back straight and your shoulders well back.

Do not bend forward, with rounded shoulders and an enormous bow in your back – you will feel wretched because your muscles will not strengthen the way they should. Sit badly and you will feel awful.

Some people will, of course, look much better than others. If you happen to be small, your legs will not be as long as someone who is tall. It is a matter of build and there is nothing anyone can do about it. Yet a small person can look just as smart as someone with long-legs by sitting properly in the saddle, with spine straight, shoulders back, and heels down. But imagine what a short person looks like hunched up, with shoulders rounded, as though they were so tired they were about to fall asleep.

In order to sit in the saddle properly, you must grip with your thigh muscles and knees, while the lower parts of the legs are used as aids to kick the horse or pony on when you want him to move off, or to help instruct him in the way you want to go – to the left or to the right. And when I say kick, I do not mean a thumping great wallop. Use just enough pressure so that he still feels comfortable and yet receives the message that you want him to obey the instruction.

All too often you see people with their legs right off the saddle, bobbing about like demented monkeys, losing all control. If their mounts did suddenly leap into their strides those on top would be left waggling their legs in fresh air. Always retain contact with your mount and use your bottom to urge him forward by pressing down into the saddle and forward with your stomach muscles.

For very young riders things are somewhat different, because they will not have the strength or the ability early on to manage most of the points mentioned here. They will probably need to be on a lead rein and they should use what are called safety stirrups. These mar-vellous irons have been designed with the young, inexperienced rider in mind, so that if they do happen to fall off they will not get their feet caught up in the stirrup and be dragged. Safety stirrups are similar to ordinary everyday ones, except that instead of metal outer edges they have a strip of rubber which clips on, and which will come off in the event of an accident. It is an ingenious device which has more than proved its worth over the years.

I would like to add here that no child who has just started riding should ever be allowed to learn how to mount without being supervised by someone who knows what they are doing. If they learn all the wrong things to begin with, it can take a long time to teach them the correct methods. So, if you go to a riding school and have not had lessons beforehand, ask for someone experienced to be on hand to make sure you are doing things properly. That way you will learn, and enjoy yourself because the plain fact is, learning can be enormous fun.

One other important rule to observe concerns the stirrup bar – the bar on the saddle on which the leather fits. This bar, which is hinged, must always be down; if it is locked up, and you should fall off, the stirrup leather will not come free from the saddle and you could be dragged, with obvious consequences.

Also, it is advisable periodically to swap your leathers from one side of the saddle to the other. This is because mounting stretches the nearside leather and if the same one is used all the time, you will finish up with one leather longer than the other.

7

Trotting, cantering and jumping

When you first start to trot you will find that it is one of the hardest movements of all to get used to and, in the very early days, there will be times when you want to give it up altogether. It can make you tired, sore and very frustrated. But persevere because the movements will come eventually, and once you have mastered them you will enjoy a keen sense of achievement.

To begin with I shall deal with the rising trot, which is the most usual one for everyday riding. If you are just beginning you should really learn on a lunge rein, since the person on the other end can control the horse, point out your mistakes and help you to correct them. Riding on the lunge in an enclosed school or paddock is by far the safest way to learn. This way you will get used to trotting the horse on both the left leg and the right. In equestrian terms these are known as the nearside and offside. To start the trot, you squeeze with your legs. When the horse responds you must rise in the saddle and count 'one, two'. In time with his movements. The trot is simply a two-time beat and if you count as you go along it will help you adjust to the horse's movements.

At first you will miss some of the beats and bounce around but try and regain the rhythm and keep in time with your mount. It is hard, and it will take a lot of practice. But the person on the end of the lunge will prevent the horse taking off with you. He or she will also change the direction occasionally, which is important because while you are learning, and doing the same things over and over again, the pony or horse can become bored. Therefore things should be made as interesting for him as possible.

Don't be rough on his mouth

When you first learn to trot you may find yourself tempted to keep your balance by gripping hold of the reins tightly and tugging at them. You must avoid this because you will pull the animal's mouth about and will end up relying on the reins for balance. You should keep yourself in place in the saddle by gripping with your knees, and rising and falling in rhythm with the horse's front leg movements. It is a good idea to fit a neck strap which you can hold on to if you feel the need.

The horse moves his legs in diagonal pairs when he trots and in time you will be able to recognize which diagonal he is on as your seat touches the saddle. When you can do this remember to change the diagonal from time to time. If your weight is always in the saddle when one particular diagonal pair of legs is on the ground you run the risk of straining the horse's legs and making him 'one-sided'.

The sitting trot is totally different from the rising trot because your seat does not leave the saddle. You merely grip with your knees and thighs and sit deep in the saddle to stop yourself bouncing about. Practising this movement gives you independence of the reins, and in time will strengthen your legs to such a degree, that you will not find trotting tiring. After a while, you will notice that you become relaxed and your muscles will begin to cope without too much trouble. But it does take time and a lot of patience on your part.

Remember to keep your back straight, but not rigid, and your shoulders back, and breathe normally all the time. This will help you cope with the strain and you will be amazed how quickly everything becomes easier. Being tense when riding is no good at all and terribly tiring. In my opinion, trotting is the hardest part of learning to ride but, once you have conquered it, you will thoroughly enjoy going out for a ride and will be full of confidence, and safe. It does take lots of time though and you must not give up, even if you think that you might never be able to trot properly.

Once you have mastered the trot it will be time for you to be taught how to canter, and this can sometimes be somewhat unnerving because the pace you have been used to will increase slightly and the movements of the horse or pony will be quite different. The hardest thing of all, perhaps, is going from the trot to the canter because some mounts, particularly if they are old and sluggish, prefer to remain at the slower pace and keep trotting no matter what. Getting such a horse to canter is good experience because it makes you use your legs as aids.

The person teaching you will probably take the lesson in a paddock, large enough for constructive movement but not so big that you could be run away with once the lunge is removed. Never think that because you can trot you will automatically be able to canter; even if you find you can, you will not at first know how to keep your mount collected and balanced.

You do not go from a walk straight into a canter because that can sometimes prove dangerous, particularly when you are out riding, and there are several other people with you.

Ponies, like young people, sometimes get excited when they are together, and they must be taught the right way to do everything at the start. The transition from trot to canter takes thinking about and, in some cases, requires a fair amount of tact. First, get your pony going smoothly in sitting trot. The best way to make the transition to canter is when the pony is going into a bend. If you are on a left-handed one, you can urge him to canter by sitting in the saddle and using your left leg on the girth and right leg slightly behind the girth to make him strike off with the near fore. Once your mount starts cantering move your body with the rhythmic three-time beat of the canter. At first you may find that instead of maintaining the beat, he slows down and breaks back into a trot, leaving you wondering how on earth you are going to get him going again. Simply talk to him, sit at the trot as you did before, and then urge him once again with your legs to canter. It will not hurt him and the instruction, if applied correctly, will be obeyed. When turning to the left at the canter the horse must lead with his nearside foreleg; but remember to change to the right lead every few minutes, so that he does not tire of the same movements and become bored.

If you are cantering in a circle to the left and want to go in the opposite direction, return to trot and change direction by going diagonally across the paddock, and then turning the other way. Use your legs to ask for the correct lead, i.e. to circle to the right, right leg on the girth, left leg behind the girth. Do not try to get a horse or pony to change legs and direction in one movement; it takes time and experience and at this early stage you will not be ready to cope with it. Once you have cantered to the left, and then to the right, and feel confident and comfortable, it is time for you to start the movements you have been practising all over again. Riding properly takes a great deal of time and effort and only practice makes perfect. When you first start to canter your bottom will probably leave the saddle more than it should, and you may think you will never be able to sit to the canter like everyone else. But it will come.

Learning to canter is one thing, being able to stop is another. When you want your mount to halt, do not be rough on his mouth. Just ease gently back on the reins, keeping your hands low and pressing the weight of your body into the stirrup irons at the same time. If he refuses to pull up when you want him to, do not panic, just keep turning him in a circle and keep your mind free of everything else. It will be difficult and you may want to jump off or scream, particularly if he gets faster and faster. But concentrate on keeping calm, continue to circle him and he will eventually come to a halt and you will be safe. If you panic, you might fall off and hurt yourself.

It is an awful feeling when your horse or pony refuses to do what he is asked, but if you do not remain calm and in control of your own thoughts, the whole thing can become highly dangerous. Horses do not bolt very often, but if and when they do, you should be prepared. If you own a horse who takes off at the least provocation, and keeps on doing so, sell him at once and tell whoever is buying him that he is too strong for you and needs someone more experienced in the saddle. Keeping a horse who runs off or takes charge regularly is a waste of time and will make your life a misery.

The majority of horses and ponies, however, have tremendous patience and will do exactly as you instruct them to do, which is why it is up to you to treat them with respect and not pull them about, or hurt them.

When you first start to canter you should keep the pace moderate, with your horse completely under control. When you have done that and feel you want to go a stage further, it is time to try an extended canter. This is the time when you have to be careful, because some horses try to break into a gallop and you do not want that to happen at this stage. An extended canter can only be done down the long side of a good sized paddock – at least 60m.

Do not rush your mount into an extended canter, just build up to it slowly until he is moving at the pace you want, and keep yourself and your mount balanced at all times. Move the bottom half of your body in rhythm with his, keeping your hands down and your elbows tucked into your sides. If you stick your elbows out like wings, your hands will turn in and the weight of the horse's head will hang on your wrists. This is not only wrong, but tiring as well.

Galloping is merely an extension of the canter, but when you are just starting to ride it is best to keep to trot and canter before attempting to gallop. Once you have gained experience, going faster becomes automatic and will not be dangerous because by then you will have enough knowledge to know exactly what is required, and what to do, at any given moment. Galloping before they are ready is a mistake many riders make, and it can be a harrowing experience if things go wrong and the horse takes off and maybe gets the bit between his teeth.

The art of good riding is to take everything one step at a time and to learn all you possibly can about controlling and working a horse. That way you feel comfortable and when he sets off he does so on the right leg and obeys the instructions you are transmitting to him. You will not learn this in five minutes. It takes a great deal of time and effort on your part, and galloping about all over the place should be the furthest thing from your mind in the early stages of your training. There is so much pleasure in being able to trot and canter properly, and turn and stop when you want, that everything else is a bonus.

Once you have mastered the movements I have discussed, it is time to move on and learn how to jump. And, by that, I do not mean that within a few weeks you are going to be proficient enough to ride at a show. Indeed, you will be spending several weeks doing things you might well find boring and unnecessary; but I can assure you that the only way to learn is to take time and put a great deal of effort into what you are doing. Otherwise you might as well not bother to ride because only those who care for their horse and themselves, in that order, have any right to be in the saddle.

I will assume that you have progressed enough to know what you are doing with your horse, and that you have control of him and are ready for the next stage of tuition. Even so, learning to jump should be done under the watchful eye of an expert. Jumping is great fun if done correctly and all you need to start with is access to a paddock and several showjumping poles. Place the poles in a straight line spaced out at intervals of 2.7m. Walk your horse around the poles and then over them. He will look at them at first, but just squeeze him on with your legs to encourage him to walk over them.

Do this several times and then space the poles 1.3m apart, but not in a straight line; this time put them in a wide semi-circle, then go back to the start of the semi-circle and trot over them. You might think that putting down the poles at certain distances apart is a bore, and you will certainly be tempted to drop them down at random. But do not, because the distances have been worked out to make the exercise safe and easy for the horse; they correspond with the average horse's stride at walk and trot and if you do not pay attention to such details, you will find your horse stepping on the poles, or jibbing at them.

That defeats the object for both you and your horse, so put the poles down at the distance stated. If you find that your horse has a long stride then the poles can be altered slightly to accommodate that. Normally, though, the spaces suggested between the poles should be ideal. With this particular training session the object is to make you and your horse confident going over small obstacles and to make it as comfortable for both of you as possible.

Remember, whatever you do, do not rush him into or over the poles, just go at a nice balanced pace at both walk and trot.

Look straight ahead, not down at the poles or at your mount's legs; if you look down you will unbalance him and you might cause him to make mistakes. It is all a question of confidence, and that will only come with practice and doing everything the way it should be done. There are no short cuts. It all takes time.

When you have mastered going over poles on the ground at walk and trot it is time to take the jumping lesson a step further and to raise the poles off the ground slightly to a height of 20cm. Then you should trot over them. When you are doing these exercises you should be using the 'forward' seat, at both trot and canter, gripping firmly with your knees at all times. Do not flop about in the saddle, or bounce up and down like a yoyo. Every movement must be calculated and precise, and you must practise until you can do everything properly.

If you are learning to jump your horse at a riding school, the person who is helping you will have access to cavalletti, and after the poles exercise you will progress to these small jumps. Cavalletti are poles which lie lengthways between small cross poles at each end, and are ideal for the exercises you are practising. When riding you will sometimes hear words that you do not fully understand but do not be put off, just ask someone what they mean.

When learning to jump remember never to overface yourself or your horse; everything should be taken in stages and if you feel you are taking on too much at one time, stop and wait for another day. It does not matter how long you take to become good at what you are doing, as long as you get it right eventually. If you start by thinking you will be able to jump anything put up in front of you within a few weeks, you had better revise your opinion, because it takes months of constant practice and study to become even half good.

Many people recommend that when you are tackling small obstacles like poles on the ground and cavalletti, you should do so with your feet out of the stirrups to strengthen your leg muscles. But for the absolute novice I do not recommend this at all. Keep your feet in the stirrup irons at all times, because that is what they are there for, and if you want to build up your leg muscles, do it by everyday exercise. Try walking or cycling up hills, or lying on your back in your room at home, lifting one leg up into the air and then the other. Also practise sitting in your saddle on a wooden saddle horse at the stables if they have one.

You will also find that when out riding if you stand in the stirrup irons and grip with your knees at the walk or trot, your muscles will soon develop and be good enough for what you want to do when jumping. It is all a matter of opinion, and having ridden since I could walk and watched many riders in action all over the world, I would advise you to keep your feet in the stirrup irons when riding.

Next ask your helper to put a single cavalletti at the end of your line of poles, about 3m from the last one. Then go back to the start of the course, trot over the poles and canter over the cavalletti. The whole point of this exercise is to get you and your horse thinking about what you are doing; once you have trotted over the final pole on the ground, gather your horse, squeeze with your legs, push with your seat and make him canter over the cavalletti.

When first doing this you might find that your mount attempts to trot over the cavalletti as he did the poles. If this does happen do not worry unduly because it is only natural for him to do this if you have failed to give him the correct instruction on the approach to the jump.

Have several more attempts until you both get it right; when you do, it is the most wonderful feeling and one you will remember for a long time after. But you will make many mistakes, become terribly frustrated and at times believe that you are never going to manage to jump a horse properly for as long as you live. That is normal and many others before you have experienced the same thing so forget it, and get on with the job in hand. Learn to be proficient through hard work, concentration and dedication.

When you have practised over the poles on the ground, leading to the single cavalletti, remove the poles from the training area and concentrate on the cavalletti alone. This will prove to be somewhat harder than the other lessons because you will not have the poles to give you a line to the jump. Firstly, canter around the obstacle one way, and then the other, until you feel that your horse is moving well for you and is calm and relaxed. Then, without stopping, approach the cavalletti at the canter and jump it. You might find that your mount has a good look at it beforehand but do not worry too much. Try it again, looking straight ahead, and encourage the horse to canter into the centre of the jump. A short distance from the obstacle count 'one, two, three', and be ready to incline the top half of your body forward to help him after he has left the ground.

The movement happens very quickly and you must think as fast as you can. If you do not, when the horse takes off, you will rock backwards and lose the all-important balance you and your mount need to negotiate the obstacle correctly.

Keep practising over the single cavalletti until you feel confident enough to put more of them up and progress slowly but surely in height. The key to it all is timing, balance, approach and learning to see the right stride before take off. It will all come right in the end if you apply yourself to the work involved, and you will be the best judge as to when you should try slightly bigger jumps.

8
Keeping your horse or pony safe

Practically every day a pony or horse goes missing in Britain, leaving the owners heartbroken and wondering what on earth they are going to do to get their animal back safely, or what they could have done to prevent the thieves taking him in the first place. It is an awful dilemma but the fact is that looking after the safety of your horse is as important as looking after yourself in the saddle. You can only take so many precautions but that is better than not taking any at all.

The number of horses which go missing from their fields or stables is increasing each year, and although the police try their hardest their job is not an enviable one and more often than not they cannot solve many of the cases. That is not a reflection on them because, after all, where do you start to look for a stolen horse or pony? Unless somebody saw the thieves and made a note of the lorry or horsebox they used to spirit the animal away, it is almost impossible for the police to trace them.

They do not give up though, but try their hardest to find stolen animals. They know what the owners are going through and make as many checks as they can. But the police obviously cannot spend too much time and effort, when they have so few leads, and they do not have an inexhaustible army of men and women to send to all parts of the country in search of missing horses.

So although you must always report any stolen horses to the police immediately, it helps their fight against crime if you take sensible precautions against horse thieves. One of the best ways to do this is to have your horse or pony freeze marked by FarmKey

Ltd, a Banbury-based company.

They have had many years of experience and much success in retrieving stolen horses and ponies. For those of you who have never heard of the company or do not know what freeze marking is, I will explain in detail.

Many people have their horses and ponies branded, but freeze marking is unlike traditional methods of hot branding, hoof marking or lip tattooing. A super-chilled marker is applied to a clipped part of the horse's skin, usually on the left side of the saddlepatch. This kills the pigment cells in the hair, which re-grows white within a few weeks. When the hair has grown it produces a distinctive and permanent mark on the animal which can then be instantly recognized by the owners, and by traders, auctioneers and the police. When the saddle is placed on the horse the freeze number is invisible. It is a brilliant idea and has proved highly successful. If your horse or pony is grey, or white, that does not present a problem: the marking is done by the same method as for other coloured horses, but produces a bald mark.

FarmKey have thought of everything. They mark each animal with its own number, which is then recorded in a register. This information can, if necessary, be made available to police forces throughout the country seven days a week, twenty-four hours a day, which helps them enormously when they are searching for a stolen horse or pony.

Freeze marking is a humane method of putting a permanent mark on a horse, and is a tremendous way of making sure that whoever tries to steal your mount thinks very hard about it before doing so; indeed, if he has any sense at all, he leaves well alone.

All the genuine people connected with the horse world are angry about horse stealing, because they know what the owners go through when an animal they love is taken away from them. So, if they are offered a horse which has been marked, they will not only refuse to buy it until ownership has been proved, but will also report any suspicious person to the police as quickly as possible.

Rustlers know this can happen and that is why most of them keep well away from horses who have been freeze marked or branded. There are occasions when those particular animals do go missing, but many have been found and then returned to their owners. The

Get friends to watch your horse

point is that if you did not have a specific identification mark on your mount, how could you possibly hope to find him again unless you happened to discover him personally? You can, of course, give the description of him to the police but, alas, many horses look alike, and what are the chances of a policeman in Wales, say, recognizing a horse stolen in Scotland or any other place? There are thousands of chestnut horses with a star on their forehead and a white sock. Does the policeman apprehend everyone seen with a chestnut horse with a white star? No, of course not, and that is why freeze marking is so important. The four figure numbers can easily be recorded in a notebook and all it takes is for the policeman to flick through it, checking the numbers against those which have been recorded in the national security register. He can tell at once if a particular horse is the one he is looking for.

This saves the hard worked police a lot of wasted time and unnecessary effort. And when you consider how much crime takes place in Britain every day of the week, having even the minutest detail noted is a bonus for them. In fact, the police back the freeze marking system, as do the British Horse Society, because they know how helpful and important it is and that it can save many problems later on if your horse or pony does go missing.

The first question people ask themselves when considering having their horse freeze marked is 'Will it hurt my horse?' It is not painful and in fact is the most humane way of going about the job. Another point they ask to be clarified is 'Will I be able to ride the animal as soon as it is done?' FarmKey recommend that the horse should not be ridden for three days afterwards. If the animal happens to have a sensitive skin you might even wait a little bit longer, but surely it is worth it. It is also recommended that after the mark has been put on you place a numnah or cloth under the saddle until the white hair has grown through. In the case of a bald marked horse, the company advise the use of a cloth or numnah at all times.

One of the bonuses of having freeze marking done is that some insurance companies will give you reduced rates which, in the long run, can save you a lot of money. They also see the value of the system and know that it is a good thing to have. While mentioning saving money, it is also wise to note that if you have your horse marked in a group, it is cheaper than having someone visit your yard to do a single horse. If you are thinking about having it done, contact your local riding school and ask if anyone else is interested, because that way you will all save money.

What happens if your horse has been freeze marked and then goes missing? The first thing to do is to make contact immediately with the police and tell them what has happened; then phone FarmKey, who notify ports, slaughterhouses and the horse sales, and also keep in touch with the police. This system, along with the fact that the company offers a £2000 reward for anyone helping to convict a horse thief, has met with great success in the past. Apart from anything else, it makes you feel a lot better because you are doing something constructive which might eventually lead to your mount being returned. There is nothing worse than to be sitting at home when your horse has gone, worrying about what to do next. Knowing that FarmKey and the police are on your side can be a great comfort. They also keep in touch and let you know how everything is going. They know it is a terrible time and do their best to ease the situation for you.

Losing a dear equine friend can be a harrowing experience. I can remember one lady who phoned me at the *Daily Mail* in tears when her horse went missing, asking me to write a story about the theft and offering a £500 reward for the return of the horse. She was sad and even travelled the country looking for the animal, visiting sales, phoning abattoirs and generally seeking information anywhere about the horse. This particular lady was very lucky because the animal was eventually found not very far from where she lived, having been stolen by a local person. And she did not have to pay any reward money.

There may be occasions when, no matter what you do, or how careful you are, you will not stop the rustlers taking, or trying to take, what belongs to you. They do not consider what it does to you or the animal you have kept and loved for many years. All they are interested in is making money and they do not care how they do it. In short, they are hard people.

Often they will try to sell off the animal at a show, or privately, as quickly as possible, in order to save the expense of keeping him. There are some people who would buy without asking too many questions, but many would inform the police if they thought something was wrong.

The sad thing about today's rustlers is that many of them steal horses and ponies to sell for meat. This particular subject might make you feel disgusted but, alas, many people abroad like to eat horse meat and whenever there is a market, someone, somewhere, will supply the goods.

Horses come under the hammer in their hundreds at sales around the country and the people who are buying them are meat wholesalers. It is quite legal and they are entitled to earn a living, no matter how awful you and I think it is.

But the sales officials on the whole are reputable men and if a horse is freeze marked or branded they can fairly easily find out who the real owners of the animal are; and if the police, or FarmKey, have supplied them with the number marks of the horses they are looking for, the chances are the villans will be apprehended and brought to justice.

Never assume that your horse is safe and that thieves would not be interested in him because, perhaps, he is old and really just a pet.

One of the best precautio s you can take when trying to beat the rustlers is to keep an ever watchful eye on your mount. If he lives in a field away from your home make sure that you visit him every day, twice a day if possible. That means that if the thieves are watching your horse they will realize there is always somebody likely to be around. It might just persuade them to forget the idea altogether or, at the very least, to go somewhere else and leave you and your horse alone. When visiting your pony to see if he is safe, make sure that you change the times of the visits so that nobody can pin-point exactly when you will turn up. If you do not follow a set pattern, it means the rustlers cannot either. Thieves love people who are predictable because it helps to make their filthy job that much easier. Another thing for you to remember is that those who steal to live are not, and never will be, gentlemen. They take what they want when they want and only your vigilance, and the police, can stop them.

Crooks do not like hassle and if something can be made easy for them that is how they like it, but if you make everything hard for them by constructive thinking they might just leave you and your horse alone.

Their favourite place to steal from is a field which lies beside or near a road, where their horsebox or trailer can be driven in or alongside, and the luckless horses loaded up without too much trouble.

The strange thing is that if people see a horsebox parked outside a field the majority automatically assume that it belongs to the owners of the horses in that field.

If more people were to question the actions of others and inform the police if they think something at all suspicious, perhaps more horses and ponies could be saved from being stolen. It might also save a good many lives.

If you cannot make the journey to the field where you keep your pony twice a day to check up on him, then see if anyone who lives nearby will keep an eye on things for you. That way you increase his safety chances and if the person who is helping you out sees something unusual all they need to do is inform the local police, who will investigate. Remember, though, that it is not this person's responsibility if anything does go wrong. This can only be used as a back-up to what you are prepared to do yourself.

To help the horse and to cut down the work the police might be required to do, it is always wise to have the strongest lock possible on the gate of the field in which you keep your mount. The best way to lock up the gate is to have a large chain which wraps around the post several times and then is secured by a padlock. At least then if the rustlers try to break in, they are going to have a job on their hands undoing the chain and trying to break the padlock. That could easily cause a great deal of noise and attract the attention of people nearby who might, just might, think that something is wrong if they see a man hitting a gate with a sledge hammer!

A few years ago it was almost unheard of for young people to have their horses stolen, for meat or for any other reason, but nowadays it is a regular occurrence, which every decent person is trying hard to stamp out. But unless the correct precautions are taken, and while people, young and old, continue to make things easy for the thief, it will go on and on and, if anything, grow. All too often I have seen dozens of horses grazing in fields and, although they have an ample supply of food and water, there very rarely appears to be anyone at all interested in them until they feel like a ride. Well, if you behave like that you are inviting trouble because of your laziness. I know as you grow older your love of ponies and horses might wane, but the animals are your responsibility while you own them and it is up to you to make sure that their welfare is uppermost in your mind.

The big trouble with girls is that when they reach the age of eighteen or nineteen many of them start to think of boys, if they have not already done so, and the poor horse which was once a prized possession suddenly gets pushed into the background and, on some occasions, forgotten about altogether. You can sometimes get away with that if your parents are horsey, or you have a brother or sister who takes over the role you once played, but if there is nobody, or your family is disinterested, then the responsibility must fall fairly and squarely on your shoulders.

You must not run away from that responsibility because your horse and pony will suffer. If you do not care, and leave him alone, then you are giving the rustler an open invitation to come and raid the field in which your horse lives. There are of course other reasons why you must not neglect him; he needs constant attention in case of illness, or lack of food and water, and all horse owners must be aware of that. No matter how much you love your boyfriend, the horse comes first. The simple fact is that the horse relies on you totally and if you forget him, or neglect him, he can do nothing at all about it. Have girlfriends or boyfriends by all means, but never, ever forget that equines are the number one priority when they are in your care.

Another danger time is when you outgrow a pony and cannot ride him anymore because of his inability to carry your weight. Either sell the animal on to someone who is caring, or make sure that you continue to give him the good life he has become used to. Do not discard him when he has done his job. Keep him safe and happy, otherwise the rustlers might take him – and why shouldn't they, if you just do not care about him any more? Face up to the pressures of ownership, take care of your pony, even if you cannot ride him, and have him freeze marked and the number recorded on the national register to keep him safe.

For information on freeze marking all you have to do is write to FarmKey Ltd, Banbury, Oxon, and ask them any question relevant to the safety of your horse or pony. They will be only too pleased to help. Remember, however, to enclose a self-addressed stamped envelope for the reply.

If we all think safety, the chances are that our horses will be safe and the rustlers eventually forced out of business.

9

Picking up legs and cleaning feet

A good friend of mine once said about horses, 'The reason I do not go anywhere near them is that they kick at one end and bite at the other.' Logical and true because, for the unwary or the uncaring, teeth and hooves can prove highly dangerous. It is vital for you to know exactly what you are doing when dealing with horses and ponies.

The first thing to learn is to talk to them when you approach them or are in their company; this puts them at ease and instils confidence. And, whenever you want to pick up one of your mount's feet, start by giving him a pat on the neck and making a fuss of him. This takes a little extra time but it could save you a lot of unhappiness later on.

Like children, horses and ponies need to be made a fuss of; and they do not like quick, jerky movements because they find them frightening. Some of them, too, are unsure of what you want and if you leap into the stable and make a dive at a horse's legs, the chances are he will pick one of them up and kick you in self-defence.

So never, ever, under-estimate the importance of being careful and concerned about what you are doing. Horses can think, but not as quickly as you; and although you might know exactly what you want an animal to do, he may not feel like doing it, or simply cannot understand the meaning of your instructions. So, to begin with, once you have entered the stable make friends with him, pat his neck, rub an ear and give him a pat on the rump. It will be appreciated.

Picking up your horse's feet is a regular job so it makes sense to

You must always pick out a horse's feet before and after a ride

The easy way to mount is to be given a leg-up

Never sit down when grooming a horse's legs — squat so that you can move quickly if necessary

Above   Before mounting, make sure the stirrup leathers are about the right length like this

Below   Tighten the girths but make sure they are not twisted underneath the horse's stomach

Put left leg in the stirrup . . .

stand in the saddle . . .

swing right leg over . . .

then sit safely and comfortably

Above A collecting ring at a show. Check when it's your turn to compete by looking at the board. A helper will chalk up your number

Below Riding on a bridlepath. Make sure there is a suitable distance between your horse and the one in front when riding in Indian file

learn to do it properly. If you frighten your horse, your appearance in the stables each morning will be a test of strength between you and him – and you will be the loser.

To pick up either of the forelegs, stand facing the animal's tail. Before you begin the task of raising the feet, run your hand down the horse's shoulder, give him a pat, and then continue the movement down to the back of his knee. By this time he will have a good idea of what you want and when you go to lift the foot he will, or should, pick it up for you to examine. It is a good idea to give a firm but quiet command of 'lift' or 'up' at the same time.

If you are picking up the near fore (left) you should be using your left hand, and for the off fore (right) you should use your right hand. All these points matter a great deal. They are all designed with your safety in mind and have been tried and trusted over the years. Never ever sit or kneel in the vicinity of your horse's feet, no matter how sure you are of him, because if something startles him, he may kick out, or trample you. The lowest position you should adopt, around the horse's legs, is a crouch. From this position you can move fairly swiftly.

You must remember, too, that when you are picking up the forelegs, your hand must run down the *back* of the leg. If the animal thrusts his leg forward, your hand will not be hurt in any way. If you were to hold the front of it, your hand would be pushed forward with the force of the horse's movement and might be injured.

When picking up the hind legs, again face the animal's tail and run your hand slowly, and gently, down the front of the hind leg. If it is the nearside one use the left hand, and if the offside, the right hand. Pick the foot up and examine it. The reason for holding the hind legs from the front is that if the horse kicks back, he will not hit your hand. These are all safety measures which do not take a lot of learning and, after a while, you will start to do them automatically. Never take chances where horses and ponies are concerned; one mistake on your part, and you could regret it for the rest of your life.

Remember that horses, and even small ponies, are much stronger than you, and when dealing with them you must understand there is always a risk involved. Thinking ahead decreases the chances of injury.

There are several reasons why, at some stage, you will want to

Don't walk on rough surfaces

pick your horse's feet up and look at them. One of the main reasons is to make sure his feet are in good order. You will need to pick them up before every ride to clean them out and, therefore, you do not want trouble every time you do. Anyone who does not pick their horse's feet out regularly is heading in the wrong direction because so many things can go unnoticed and eventually make him lame.

As I have already mentioned, a common ailment of the foot is thrush, which is caused by whoever is looking after the animal completely neglecting his feet. Horses get thrush as a result of standing for too long on wet bedding, so that the feet are permanently soaked, or from being constantly dirty, and never cleaned. You will know if your horse has it because it emits a disgusting smell from the frog area of the foot. Look after the feet properly and there will be little chance of your horse suffering from thrush. It is an awful affliction, made worse because you will know that it is your fault. So check the animal's feet every day and clean them out regularly.

One of the most common causes of lameness is when stones become caught between the frog and the bar of the foot and either cut into the rubbery substance of the frog, or bruise or puncture the sole. A mount with an injured foot can be out of action for a long time, so it pays to check the feet regularly to make sure the horse's soles are free of small stones, or anything else which is likely to make him lame.

It can be dangerous to go riding, having not bothered to check your horse's feet before mounting, because he might suddenly go lame, and stumble. If the ground is uneven and he trips, he might well unship you. And do not think that, even if you are just at the walk, you will not be hurt because even the slightest of falls can lead to broken bones.

To imagine how your horse feels just think of yourself with a pebble in your shoe being asked to walk along the pavement. It would not be any pleasure. And if your mount has a stone lodged in his hoof, it hurts him in just the same way. He could, of course, step on and pick up stones or flints during your ride. If this happens, pick up the foot and dislodge the stones with your hoofpick. You should only ever carry a folding hoofpick when riding in case you fall off. If you carry the ordinary kind and you take a fall, the metal could stick into your leg.

Horses can of course go lame for other reasons. Like you, their feet grow, and they need to be re-shod and have their hooves trimmed at regular intervals. Depending on the amount of work they are doing, they will need new shoes about every five or six weeks. The main reason for this is because if the shoes were not changed they would pinch and the horse could develop corns. Shoes also need to be changed when they wear thin. Even a horse which is not being ridden at all needs attention from the blacksmith every six to eight weeks, because the hooves will still need trimming.

There are two types of shoeing, hot shoeing and cold. If your horse has been looked after by the same blacksmith for a long time he will know the size of shoe the horse requires and, once they have been made, he can replace the old ones at any time with ready made shoes. To begin with, however, he needs to make a shoe that will fit your horse exactly, and for that he will shape it in his forge using the hot shoe method. This means he puts the iron for the shoe in the fire and works it until he has it right. Once he has done this, he records the size and will know exactly what is required any time your mount needs to have his shoes replaced.

Shoes are held on by nails, whose points are driven through the insensitive wall of the hoof and then turned over at the ends to keep the shoes in place. Sometimes, however, the nails become loose and the ends (called clenches) push themselves away from the outer wall of the hoof and need to be hammered back into place or replaced. This must be done properly, otherwise when you go to lift up the hoof they could cut your fingers. They must be secured properly for other safety reasons. If the nails work loose, the shoes could come off, or twist around and cut the horse's own feet. Stepping on a twisted shoe can be extremely painful for the horse and can cause severe lameness.

If the shoe twists it must be pulled off by the blacksmith or, if you have been taught how, by yourself. If you left it the nails would puncture the sole of the foot and it could put your mount out of action for weeks, and cause him a lot of pain. Blacksmiths are worth their weight in gold and the days when you could employ inexperienced or unqualified people are rapidly disappearing, thank goodness. Now they have to take and pass stringent tests; those who do not come up to scratch do not pass.

A good blacksmith enjoys his work and takes pride in it. He knows what can happen if he makes a mistake, or is unsure of what he is doing. Just one nail hammered into the wrong part of the hoof, or too much horn cut off the toe, can make a horse lame for a long time. That is why the blacksmith must know exactly what he is doing and why it takes years of patience and practice to learn the trade.

Yet although there are many youngsters who want to train as blacksmiths there was a time, and maybe still is, when qualified people were loath to take boys and girls on and teach them the trade. The main reason for this was the fact that they had to pay them and allow them time off to go to college, knowing that they could not earn their keep for some time because they could not be asked to shoe a horse with the limited experience they had.

I can understand that situation and have a certain amount of sympathy with the blacksmith. Yet how do we replace the existing ones when they retire, and make sure that there are always plenty of blacksmiths available, if there is a reluctance to train them?

Even in this day and age when horses are used mainly for pleasure and not, as in times gone by, for work, we cannot do without good, caring blacksmiths. It is, however, very hard work and the job also carries enormous responsibility. Only the most dedicated ever make it in the trade and only the best keep going.

There are times when the blacksmith's knowledge can save horses from certain death, or at least help to make their lives much easier. Sometimes when a horse or pony goes lame the vet cannot, no matter how he tries, find the reason and so cannot cure the problem. That is no fault of his because the foot is difficult to treat and there are only a certain number of things that can be done.

Let us say, for example, that the vet recommends that the shoes of your horse be raised so that, for a short time, all pressure is taken off the frog or heel – only the blacksmith would know exactly how it should be done. He would also know that the treatment could not go on for too long because, without the normal amount of pressure on the frog, the condition of the animal's feet would soon start to deteriorate.

He might also recommend, if the vet has not been able to find a cure, a different form of treatment for the foot which has, on some other occasion, worked well and brought a pony back to fitness and health. A good vet will always work in very close association with a blacksmith when there is trouble in the foot, and that is a good thing because they can sometimes help each other with the result that the horse or pony recovers.

I have had personal experience of how a blacksmith can help a pony who has something other than ordinary feet, because our family pony has for years suffered from thin soles and we have to be very careful how he is worked when the ground is uneven or firm. In fact we keep well clear of all those surfaces which could make him go lame.

But because his feet have to have special attention we need to take constant advice from our blacksmith. He is one of the best there is and has looked after our pony for years, knows exactly what our pony needs and makes sure that his feet are always in good working order.

It costs me about £15 for a set of four shoes and our pony has his replaced at about six-week intervals. But if he was doing more road work, they would probably need replacing every five weeks, depending on how hard he was on the shoes. The fact is you cannot, and must not, take any chances where your horse's feet are concerned because that age old saying 'No foot – no horse' is very true.

That is why you must take every care with them. Make sure that you put hoof oil on the feet every day, because this helps to promote healthy growth and keeps them in good order. Failure to keep the hooves oiled would mean that eventually the wall of the hoof would crack or flake and that could also lead to trouble. Before riding pick the horse's feet out, wash off any mud from the wall of the foot and then apply hoof oil. This is all part of looking after your horse's safety and helping him to lead a normal, healthy life.

When caring for your horse's feet it is helpful to understand the complete structure of the hoof, which consists of the wall, the sole and the frog. Each part has its own specific purpose and each really relies on the others. If something goes wrong with one part of the foot, stress or injury can spread all through and cause very bad lameness.

The wall has been designed by nature to help protect the bones and the nerves inside the foot and it grows downwards. In its wild state the horse or pony does not need a blacksmith because the hoof, unprotected by shoes, automatically gets worn by constant use on the ground. But we expect our mounts to go over a lot of unnatural terrain, such as tarmac roads and concrete paths, and that is why your horse needs to be shod.

The frog is an ingenious part of the hoof, with a very important role to play. This rubbery-like substance acts both as a shock absorber and an anti-slipping device. As you can imagine what with the weight of the actual horse and your weight on his back, there needs to be something to take the pressure when the feet strike the ground. If the frog were not there it is not difficult to realize what sort of shock waves would be pounding the structure of the foot, and leg, every time the hoof came into contact with the ground. The frog takes the pressure and, because it can absorb it, the animal stays sound.

That is unless the animal is abused and worked too often, or too fast, on hard or uneven ground, especially when he is unfit. Then nothing will stop him having sore legs or bruised soles, which are very painful. And once something goes wrong in the foot, it can take a great deal of time to put right.

The frog is attached to the sole, whose main purpose is to protect the actual foot so that when the horse stands, or jumps on to something, it does not slip or hurt the inside of the hoof. The sole is not very thick and on some horses is particularly thin, and if that is the case he will not like flinty or particularly hard ground, because it will bruise the soles of his feet.

All these points must be understood for the safety and welfare of your horse, and if you cannot find out what your horse's feet are like, or do not understand, ask the blacksmith about them and make a note of what he says. That way there is no danger of your mount being asked to do something that will make him lame.

As I have said, it depends upon the amount of work your horse is doing as to how often he will need a change of shoes, but the fact is you must check his feet daily to see they are in good order. Looking after the feet is of vital importance.

If your horse throws a shoe, in or out of the stable yard, pick it up and put it in a safe place so that other horses or people do not come along and step on it. The nails have a dreadful habit of clinging to the shoe and it does not take much imagination to realize what would happen if another horse or pony trod on it. If your horse is at livery, the blacksmith will have a certain place where he works and there may well be a pile of old shoes there. So pick up your discarded one and put it with those out of harm's way.

Another good point to remember is to keep on the right side of your blacksmith and take notice of what he tells you about your horse. Blacksmiths are men of great knowledge where hooves and shoes are concerned and take a great pride in their work. Listen to them and heed their advice and you should have a sound horse for a long time. Be safe and sure.

10
Horses' health and dressing wounds

Horses and ponies do not like being unwell and it is up to their owners to look after them and make sure they are kept in good health and are free from pain and disease. It is not difficult if you think about what you are doing and are constantly aware of what is going on with your mount.

Although you should always call a vet if you are in any doubt about your horse's health, there are many small injuries and cuts you can cope with providing you do things properly.

When a horse or pony is feeling well he will look good in his coat, his ears will be pricked and he will be taking notice of everything that is happening around him. His eyes will be bright, he will step out as though he has a definite purpose in going somewhere and he might even be a little bit cheeky.

These are good signs and you should not worry if he moves a little too freely or gallops about in the paddock when you turn him loose. That is far better than his walking about with his head lowered looking utterly miserable. Look after him and he will look after you. It is a question of give and take and, as far as you are concerned, his health is of the utmost importance.

When your mount is at all unwell, he will feel awful and his ears will probably droop; he will be listless and totally disinterested in anything. His coat will be dull and he might even have that drawn-in appearance. Very much as you look and feel when you have a bad cold or the flu.

If you think your horse is unwell, take his temperature, as that is one of the best guides to his health. A horse's normal temperature is

Watch for signs of illness

100.5°F (38°C) although this might vary slightly from horse to horse.

To take a horse's temperature, insert the thermometer into his rectum and hold it there for about thirty-five or forty seconds. Make sure that you have a firm hold on it because the animal might contract the rectum muscles and draw in the thermometer. If you find that it does not insert easily, put a little vaseline on the top of the instrument. Before attempting to take his temperature, tie the horse to the string on the stable ring and, if possible, have someone hold up one of his forelegs. If the animal decides to be awkward, this will help to prevent him kicking you. Always stand to one side of him when inserting the thermometer. These are normal safety methods which will save you a lot of trouble.

If you find that the reading on the thermometer exceeds 102°F (39°C), it would be wise to call the vet. When you have finished reading the instrument, clean it in cold water and dip it in Dettol. Then put it away in a safe place so that it does not get stepped on and broken. Always wash your hands properly after such an exercise to keep yourself safe and free from germs.

If you are young and inexperienced, ask an older, more experienced person to take your horse's temperature because it can be dangerous if the animal becomes frightened and kicks out.

Another guide to whether your horse is well or not is the pulse rate. This is normally between 36 and 42 beats per minute though in young animals it can be as rapid as 45 beats per minute. To take the pulse, use your fingers and feel under the lower jaw where the artery passes close to the bone. Just hold your fingers there gently (definitely not too hard) and count the pulse beat. You can also take your horse's pulse on the artery on the animal's cheek, just above and behind the horse's eye; or inside the foreleg, on a level with the elbow.

You should always have a medical kit locked away in the tack room so that you can administer first aid without wondering where on earth you are going to get the equipment you need. Ideally you should have bandages, cotton wool, gauze, safety pins, scissors, surgical tape, thermometer, vaseline, witch hazel, antiseptic, antibiotic powder, Animalintex impregnated poultice dressing, a pair of rubber gloves, clean sponges and a box in which to keep everything.

If you own a pony or horse, these are the basic requirements for your first aid kit, and they should be bought when you take charge of the animal. Once he is with you, he is your responsibility, and even if you do not think you have the experience to administer first aid yourself, the person who does it for you will need the equipment mentioned above. A vet will have his own.

Most of the time you will only be required to deal with aches and sprains and, the commonest of all injuries, small cuts on the legs. These tend to look awful when surrounded by dried blood, yet they are often nothing but slight nicks of the flesh which can be cleared up almost at once, with simple treatment.

What is of vital importance is that you make sure your horse has the necessary anti-tetanus injections because puncture wounds can cause lockjaw which is usually fatal. Your vet will give your horse the primary injections and advise you when a booster will be necessary thereafter. It is up to you to keep a veterinary record so that you know when the animal needs a booster after the initial course of injections. It is just a case of being methodical.

The germ which causes tetanus lives in the ground and gets into the horse's body by means of a wound so you can see that if your mount has not been immunised, he will stand a chance of getting tetanus. Do not take any chances - it is just not worth it.

I do not wish to frighten you but you should be aware of the symptoms of tetanus, which are easily recognizable. An affected horse will start off having general stiffness, a high temperature and will stand with his back legs thrust out and his nose pushed forward. The membranes of the eyes will cover the eyeballs and in the advance stages his jaws will lock. It really is awful - so do not take any chances.

If your horse does nick or cut himself, and it is very easily done, the first thing to do is to tie the animal to the string on the stable ring, clean the wound, cut away the surrounding hair and apply wound powder. Then cover it with lint or gauze-covered cotton wool and bandage lightly. This is to allow for any swelling that may develop from the injury: if you tie the bandage too tightly you will make things more difficult.

Sprains in horses are quite common and are caused by a multitude of things, not least of all working an unfit horse too much, or working in heavy ground. Jumping too much will also lead to sprains and pulled muscles. To prevent them, you just have to be sensible about the amount of work you give your horse. Making him twist and turn too quickly will also pull muscles and cause lameness. At all times make sure you gear his work to his degree of fitness.

If he does suffer a sprain, to bring the swelling down you should run cold water over the injury. Do this for twenty to thirty minutes, then apply a poultice, which will reduce the inflammation. If your mount hurts one of his legs, remember to put a bandage on the opposite, sound leg, because he will tend to take the weight off the damaged one and put extra stress on the other. A bandage will help support that extra load.

Even the slightest sprain can materialize into something a lot worse if treatment is not readily available, and the action I have suggested will go a long way to preventing the injury becoming worse. If the leg has not improved within the first twenty-four hours, summon the vet and let him give you a professional diagnosis.

Remember that when you use the hose on a horse you must be gentle, and start by washing the hoof so that he can get used to the water and the splashing noises that automatically go with it. You should also have greased the heel beforehand so that he does not become sore. When you have completed the hosing, dry the leg gently and put some more grease on the heel.

If you have never seen a lame horse or pony, and think you may not be able to recognize one, do not worry, because it is not difficult to detect when all is not well. If a horse goes lame, in front or behind, his stride will become uneven and this will be more noticeable when he is trotting. If you think he has lamed himself, ask someone experienced at the stables to watch him as he is first walked, then trotted out in hand; they should be able to tell right away. You will find that if he is lame in one of his hind legs, the quarters will drop more on one side than the other as he moves; if he is hurt on a foreleg, his head will nod as the sound leg hits the ground.

It is a point to note that trotting on a slight incline will also help you find lameness in a foreleg. But finding exactly where your horse is in pain is sometimes difficult and you must exercise a lot of patience.

The lameness might not be in the main body of the leg at all and you must take a good look at the foot and see if the trouble is there. He may have pricked the sole with a nail or tack. Firstly, check to see if the shoe is on properly and not twisted in any way. It should be on firmly and have no risen clenches. Secondly, check to see that there is nothing stuck in the frog or between the frog and the bar of the hoof.

Also look to see that the shoe is not pinching in any way, particularly in the toe area. It might be that the hoof has grown and his shoes are too tight. If this is the case, he will need to have the shoes removed and the horn trimmed. Or it might be the heel that is the cause of the problem. Heels can crack in very wet or frosty weather and this will cause pain if it is not treated at once.

The horse might have damaged his legs himself by what is called 'brushing'. This is when one leg strikes the other when the horse is moving and it can be extremely painful. If your horse is prone to doing this, protect his legs with brushing boots, which are fastened around the fetlock. Your blacksmith will also be able to fit him with feather-edged shoes, which will help. If he has hurt himself in this manner, clean the wound and apply antiseptic ointment.

A more serious injury can be caused by your mount over-reaching, which is exactly what the word implies. He over-reaches with his hind foot, which hits his foreleg. When this happens, bathe the wound, again apply antiseptic dressing and bandage lightly over a cotton-wool pad. This will help to keep pressure off the skin. If you were to put the bandage on too tightly, the area would swell and make him more uncomfortable.

As well as injuries to the legs, back injuries can also stop you riding your horse, and make him feel dreadful. Saddle galls, caused by the saddle not fitting correctly and rubbing the animal's skin, are very painful. It might be that the arch of the saddle tree is too narrow so that it pinches the withers and makes them sore. Or the arch may be too wide so that the saddle presses down on the horse's spine. Galls can also be caused by your not doing up the girths properly, or by sliding about a great deal in the saddle. Once the skin is rubbed sore or broken it is a long job to put it right. If you did not bother, the horse would be in a great deal of pain when you put your tack on him and rode him out. Even if the skin is not broken, you must rest the horse or pony until the hair has grown properly again. To treat this injury apply a saline solution which will help harden the area. But only use this treatment if the skin is NOT broken. If the area is raw and the skin IS broken, make a very weak saline solution, dab the area and then sprinkle sulphanilamide powder over it. Be gentle and do not rush the job. You must take the blame for this injury because your saddle should fit correctly and you should tighten the girths properly.

Your mount can also get girth galls from badly fitting or unclean girths rubbing the skin and making it raw. Again you must not ride the horse until the skin is completely healed. Some people try and put a pad under the girth, thinking that this will alleviate the pressure. That is total rubbish. Wait until the galls are healed before putting a saddle on your mount's back again.

It should never be a question of what suits you, because the health of your horse or pony must always come first, no matter how badly you want to ride. Look after him and he will look after you and you will both be safe. Take chances and short cuts and you will be heading for a great deal of trouble. Think about what you are doing and get everything right.

You may not realize it, but a bridle can cause a great deal of pain, too, particularly if the bit is rough. A rough bit will damage the horse's lips, tongue and the bars of the mouth. If he has suffered a cut, wash his mouth out and do not put a bridle on him until the cut has healed. However, it is not always a rough bit that causes damage to the mouth – it can also come about if you ride as though you were trying to stop a train, or pull on the bridle and jag his mouth. His mouth, like yours, is sensitive and must not be handled roughly. If you ride as though you have meathooks for hands, give it up and look for another hobby.

The welfare office of the British Horse Society once sent out a disturbing report concerning the way some so-called trainers were treating unbroken animals. The statement reported that some animals were having their mouths nicked at the sides with a knife, to harden them so that they would accept the bit more quickly. Apart from being morally wrong, such action is completely stupid, for, if anything, it would make the mouth so bad it would be devoid of all feeling. I do not know the motives of the people who practise such barbarities but it just goes to show how stupid and cruel some people can be.

Always treat a horse's mouth gently and he will eventually do whatever you want him to do because he will feel comfortable. Make riding him a battle and he will not enjoy having you on his back. It is all a question of give and take and of remembering you are dealing with a sensitive creature who needs proper care and consideration.

Remember that your mount can also suffer from a sore mouth if his teeth are giving him trouble; if they are rough they may cut his tongue or cheek. The cure for this is to ask the vet to come along and look at them and file any rough edges down.

When a horse gets a stomach ache it is called colic and can be very painful. It may be caused in several ways, including allowing him to take a long cold drink when he is hot or sweating, or giving him a drink after a big meal. The stomach cannot take that sort of thing without reacting in some way and it usually manifests itself in colic. It can be very painful and dangerous if not treated. It can also be caused by over-eating, crib-biting and windsucking, and taking a lot of exercise too soon after the intake of a big meal.

When you bring your horse in from exercise, if he is hot and sweating do not turn him out at once. Take time to dry him off and make him as comfortable as you can, otherwise he will catch a chill. It does not take that long to make him feel right, so make sure you do what is vital for his good health and safety.

If your horse does get colic, make sure that you do not leave him alone because he might roll in his box and become cast (stuck against the wall and unable to get to his feet again). Walk him slowly around the stable yard. This will prevent him catching a chill and to some extent take his mind off the pain he is suffering. If he does not get better quickly you *must* call the vet.

Even if you have never seen a horse with colic you will have no difficulty recognizing the symptoms because he will keep on looking round at his flanks and will sometimes try and bite them quickly, as though trying to relieve himself of the hurt. He might also stamp at the ground and try to kick the underside of his stomach. You will probably discover, too, that he has a very fast pulse rate and starts to sweat in patches. Having said that you must remember to keep him warm. The vet must be summoned and will probably administer an injection.

Another problem which can arise is your horse or pony catching a cold, particularly if he lives in. If he catches a cold he will probably find it difficult to eat his food because the lining of his throat will be sore and anything that touches it will make him cough; he may also bring food up through his nostrils. If it is a bad cold and he is feeling dreadful he will also have a mucous discharge from his nostrils.

Once one horse in a stable gets a cold it is very difficult to contain the outbreak and the only real way is to isolate the patient until he is better. You must also keep his clothes and your grooming equipment away from the other horses because germs can live in them and spread to other inmates if they come into contact with them. You will also find that his temperature will rise and you must keep him warm, though at the same time allowing him plenty of fresh air because, as you well know, there is nothing worse than having a cold, being bunged up and living in a stuffy atmosphere.

To treat a cold keep his nostrils and eyes sponged, otherwise the mucous discharge will stick to his nose and other parts of the face and make him feel even worse. Remember to destroy the swabs you use for the cleaning up operation. Do not take him out in a cold wind and do not ride him. The order for the day is gentle exercise, which will not put any strain on him. This must be done by leading him out, and when he returns make sure you rub him down and keep him warm. He must not be ridden at all until at least four days after the cold has gone. If you were to work him in this ill condition you could do him harm. What he will need is constant nursing to make him better.

Colds often produce coughing, too, but there are occasions when a horse who does not have a cold will start coughing. This could be caused by some sort of allergy, and is normally associated with his bedding. You might find that he is allergic to straw, or, indeed, to the hay he is being fed. The way to deal with this is to change his bedding and instead of using straw, try shavings, or peat or even shredded paper. Feed the minimum of hay and, if the allergy continues, consult your vet, who will take a number of tests to try and relieve, or cure the condition.

Allergies are sometimes very difficult to pin down, as some humans can testify. There are people who suffer from skin rashes the moment they come into contact with cats, dogs or horses, and others who have breathing conditions which make them wheeze if they eat certain foods. It is really a question of finding out what your particular horse cannot tolerate and keeping it away from him. But this sometimes takes time and a great deal of patience.

If you are in any doubt about your horse's health it is always wise to call in the vet and let him have a look at him. The old saying 'better safe than sorry' is so true where animals are concerned.

11
Important field checks

Too many people ride their horses and then take them to their fields and turn them out without bothering to check if they will be safe. As long as there is water available they think all is well and they can come along whenever they like, saddle up again and go for a ride. There is a lot more to it than that and it is irresponsible not to make the correct checks of the field every day.

Make sure the field is free of items such as broken glass or cans. Sadly, nowadays very few people seem to have much regard for the countryside; they think nothing of throwing away the litter they do not want, no matter how hazardous their rubbish might be to horses, ponies, cattle or sheep. The government has spent millions of pounds publicizing the issue and yet all too often you can walk in the countryside and be reminded of a rubbish tip because what should be clean, green fields or woods are messed up with cans, bottles and waste paper, left there by people who have no real right to sample the benefits of the countryside.

Because of their lack of interest, or ignorance, it is vital that you have the safety of your horse uppermost in your mind. Standing on a broken bottle can do him serious injury. It may not affect the person who dropped it there, but it will certainly make a big impact on your mount and your peace of mind. Make regular inspections of the field where your horse is kept and pick up anything that should not be there. It takes time and effort but it is something you must do daily. Do not adopt the attitude that because you did not make the mess you should not have to clear it up. That is negative thinking. Remember, the responsibility for your horse rests with you.

Rubbish can be dangerous

If he injures himself, it may well have been the fault of somebody else dropping something they should not have in his field, but it is up to you to find it before it does any harm.

But it is not only man-made rubbish which can injure your horse. Sometimes sharp stones or flints get pushed up from the earth, or are thrown into fields, and these do as much damage as glass and cans. They must be collected and disposed of at once.

Many people do not understand horses or even care about them, and some would not think twice about throwing something at them or making them race around their field for fun. It is something that only education will stop. Until people are taught why they should treat animals properly, you will continue to get the irresponsible of this world doing stupid and regrettable things. So check on your horse daily, take a good look in his field and remove anything that might harm him.

Flint, stones and glass are not the only hazards likely to be found in your horse's field. You must keep your wits about you at all times and also look for poisonous plants. There are several that are harmful to horses, one of the most dangerous being ragwort which, strangely, is more poisonous when it is dead than when it is alive. Make sure that you pull it up by the roots, remove it from the paddock and burn it. Other things poisonous to horses include yew, laburnum, deadly nightshade, acorns and bracken. If you find any of these, get rid of them at once to be on the safe side. Never take chances – be safe and your horse will be kept out of harm's way. If you do not know what these plants look like, ask someone to show you. For instance, if there is a riding school in your area, ask the person who runs it if they would be kind enough to help, or go to your local library and look at some plant books there. If you are still at all unsure about a plant, pull it up anyway and take it out of the field.

The field where you keep your horse should, ideally, be five acres if he is not getting a supplementary diet; if he is, two acres will be enough provided the grazing is good. Do not stint on this because he needs to be able to move about freely and, more importantly, he must have enough grass to eat, particularly if he is not having his food supplemented.

The best thing to do is to practise rotational grazing, whereby part of the field is fenced off and saved. Then, when the horses have cropped the grass on one area they can be moved to the good grass while the area that has been grazed has a chance to regrow. If you allow them all the grass at one time, the chances are they will just eat their way through it.

If horses and ponies live on the same area of land for any length of time, the grass will need harrowing regularly, to keep the field in good condition. Harrowing loosens and separates the earth, which in turn promotes the growth of grass. It should be done before the spring, preferably in March, and then during the summer. The chances are that not many of you will have access to a harrow, or anything with which to pull one. Well, if you do not know a friendly farmer or smallholder who has one, you will have to use a fork or a rake to maintain the land. That is hard work but it is a task which must be done if your horse is to be kept safe and well. Once the grass has been harrowed it is best to leave horses off it for a few days to give the grass time to recover. So do a section at a time.

The horses' droppings should be picked up and removed regularly in order to keep worm infestation to a minimum. All horses have worms and, although they cannot be eradicated completely, regular worming with one of the very good wormers now available will help keep the problem under control. However, there is nothing to be gained by worming your horse regularly if you leave the droppings in his field. He will just reinfest himself again when he is grazing.

Horses suffer from several types of worm. The worst is the red worm which migrates through the wall of the intestine and may cause stoppage of the blood stream. If a horse is allowed to become badly infected with red worms, it may be several months before he recovers. In very bad cases horses have been known to die, so you can see why it is so important to make sure that all is well with him. Remember, he cannot tell you how he feels, so it is up to you to think for your horse and put his needs before anything else.

As well as red worms there are whip worms, which reside in the rectum of the animal and cause dreadful irritation. This will lead to the horse constantly rubbing his tail up against the fence, or the side of his box. If he is allowed to continue doing this he will rub out the hairs of his tail and make himself very sore.

Then there is the white worm, which is one of the biggest. It is fairly long and thick and is just as disgusting as the whip and red worms.

To find out exactly what sort of worm burden your horse is carrying, take a sample of his droppings to the vet for analysis. There is nothing wrong with this, and it is not distasteful. The vet will then recommend a suitable wormer. Some animals are wormed every seven or eight weeks, but check with your vet, and he will be able to give you a routine which you can adhere to.

There is nothing nasty about worming horses and ponies. The vet will give you powders which you place in the horse's feed, or the wormer may be in the form of a paste which is easy to administer straight into the horse's mouth – it is simple and effective.

Remember, one of the surest signs of a horse who is suffering from worms, is for him to lose condition even though he has a healthy appetite.

If your horse lives out in a field he needs protection from the wind and the rain and must have somewhere to shelter from the elements. It would be cruel to expect him to live out in all weather without having a bolt hole from the rain, wind or snow. That is why a suitable shelter should be erected in the field, with an opening at the front large enough to allow two or three horses easy access. If the opening is narrow, and two or more residents try to get in at the same time, they might start kicking or biting each other. Make sure that the entrance allows plenty of room for them to manoeuvre.

The building should be sturdy so that it can cope with high winds or heavy falls of snow without any danger of falling over, or the roof caving in. If the one you have needs attention, ask a member of the family to help you put things right, or pay for someone to come and do it. It will be money well spent and will save you a lot of trouble in the long run. If the building is strong and reliable in the first place, it will last a long time and this, in turn, will save you cash, because you will not have to keep paying out for repairs or, if things are really bad, have to build a completely new one.

When your horse is being fed hay, and there are other horses in the field with him, make sure that the hay is spread out in piles a suitable distance away from each other. Horses become jealous at feeding times and are very likely to forget their manners, and try to eat their neighbour's pile of hay as well as their own. Putting the hay piles several yards away from each other prevents any kick reaching its objective.

Unlike humans, animals eat as fast as they can, when they can, and they do not particularly mind where the food comes from as long as they get their share. It is the law of nature, and nothing can change that, so you have to study their habits and work with them. You may have to protect them from themselves. Horses and ponies are somewhat like children who, no matter what good things they have, always seem to want more; wise parents make sure they do not always get their own way, but are given the things that are good for them. As far as your horse or pony is concerned it is up to you to look after him; so at feeding time make sure that he has what he should be having and does not steal the meal next door.

The field in which you keep your horse should have a good supply of water and if that water is put in a drinking trough it must be changed daily so that it is fresh and does not develop an awful green slime on the top of it, or around the receptacle that contains it. In many fields where horses and ponies are kept you see old tin cans or bath tubs used as water containers. In some cases they leak, or are liable to fall over at the slightest touch. Those water holders are useless and can be dangerous. It does not take a lot of imagination to realize what damage could be done if a heavy tub fell over on to a horse's leg or feet.

If you are using a tub for water in your field make sure that it is secure and cannot be knocked over, and also be certain that you change the water and clean the tub out at regular intervals. You would not want to drink stale, dirty water and neither does your horse. Be safe, be clean and nothing will happen to your mount. Be stupid and uncaring and allow your horse to drink bad water, and he might suffer all sorts of illness. Also remember that in hot weather horses and ponies do drink a lot and there must always be a plentiful supply for them.

You may think that there is an awful lot to remember and you are right. I do not believe in taking any chances where animals are concerned – there is always a right way to do things and a wrong way. Make sure you choose the right way, then your horse or pony will lead a good, safe life. You cannot afford to be ignorant about horses and ponies and if you want to own them, work with or be near them, you must understand their needs. There are no short cuts. It is hard work and you have got to know what you are doing. Never take the easy option about anything and always remember that slackness on your part will do your horse or pony no good at all. Think about nothing else but the comfort and safety of the animals in your care.

The ideal field in which to keep your horse is one that has a sturdy hedge around it because this not only keeps the animal in, but also helps to protect him from bad weather. The hedge must not have any gaps in it through which the horse could escape. Ideally, as an added safeguard, there should be a fence made of planks inside the hedge. If this is not available to you then strands of wire, fixed on to posts and pulled tight, will suffice. You will need at least five strands and the bottom one should be at least a foot from the ground to prevent your horse from getting a foot caught over it. This form of fencing is most certainly cheaper than post and rails, although I prefer the latter.

The whole point of erecting fencing is to keep your horse safe and inside the area where you want him to be. It is no use putting up a few strands of wire, hammered on to one or two posts, because the chances are he will push it down or knock it over and get himself caught up in the wire. Although some people advocate the use of barbed wire for keeping horses in, I totally disagree with it because there are horses and ponies who will try and jump out, and if they were caught up in barbed wire they would cut themselves badly.

If you are practising rotational grazing, which you should be doing so that the grass in your field is not all eaten up at once, it is a great temptation for your horse to try to reach the pasture which is beckoning over the other side of the fence. Horses do not understand that you are restricting their grazing for their good. They only have one aim in mind and that is to go where the grass is greener, which is always on the other side of the fence.

So you can see that it is important to have a sturdy fence, made of material which is not only going to keep your horses in, but will also prevent them from hurting themselves; they could be in a lot of trouble if they attempted to leap over into the next grassy area and failed to make the height or distance. Apart from the danger to your horse it can prove expensive to have fences which are not solid and which are in constant need of repair.

One of the best methods of keeping horses and ponies where you want them is electric fencing. If you shop around, you will find that this particular fencing is not terribly expensive. It is also good, because when you want to move the area of grazing, you need only pull up the iron posts and move them to wherever you want to go. Horses sometimes brush up against the wire and, on occasions, try to push it down, but the electrical charge which pulsates every few seconds, gives them a slight shock and they soon learn to respect the wire. The shock does not hurt them in any lasting way and as soon as they touch the wire, they back off and suffer no ill effects.

Do not try to move the fencing when the current is turned on because although it will not injure you, it is not very pleasant having an electric charge racing up your arm and it will, briefly, make you wish you had never gone anywhere near it.

One important point to remember is that the field where you graze your horse must have adequate drainage, otherwise he will be standing in water all the time, which will not do him any good. Equally, the field should not resemble a dust bowl, where the grass in next to useless and has no goodness in it at all.

One of the good things about sectional grazing is that a greedy pony will not be able to over-eat which, in the spring, when the grass is rich in nutriments, is not good for him. Allowing a pony to stuff himself so that he becomes grossly fat can lead to a condition of the feet called laminitis. This is very painful and can cause permanent damage to the feet. Ponies must have enough grass to keep them healthy, if that is their sole source of food, but never let them over-eat, because you will not be helping them.

If a pony lives out all the year round, he must have regular feeds of hay during the winter months as there is no goodness in the grass. If he is being worked, he must also have pony nuts. This food will help keep him warm and enable him to cope with bad weather conditions. You must work out the amount of food he needs yourself, because without knowing how much work the animal is doing, and how big he is, I cannot judge his requirements.

Remember, too, that in very cold weather his water supply will freeze. When that happens he cannot drink so you must make sure that the ice is broken for him. That means at least two trips a day to his field because although you might break it in the morning, it will freeze again during the evening.

His feet will need constant attention because mud and ice will cling to them and ball-up between the inner rim of the shoe and the frog. This must be picked out so that he does not bruise the soles of his feet. You might sometimes feel like staying in bed on a cold, frosty day, but your mount is your responsibility so make sure that you make those regular visits.

You might also think that there is very little danger when you turn your pony or horse out in the field. But there is, and you must always be thinking safety, for his sake and for yours. When you turn him out, do not wrap the headcollar rope around your wrist because he might get excited at the prospect of grass and attempt to pull away from you, before you are ready to let him go. Hold the headcollar rope firmly in your right hand, about five inches from the head-collar, with your left hand about six inches from the other end. That way he will be secure and, if he pulls away, you will retain control without being in danger of being dragged. When you reach the field gate, open it, close it again and walk a little way into the field, talking to your pony all the time. Make him stand for a few moments, and then release the headcollar buckle, gently slide the strap over his neck, turn and walk away.

Never encourage him to gallop off down the field and never stand waving the headcollar at him to move off. He will do so in his own time and if you were to encourage him to go dashing off at a gallop, he might slip, fall and hurt himself. He will also be that much harder to control the next time you want to release him in the field.

Never open a gate and leave it open behind you, because he would only need to side-step after you have taken off the headcollar and he could dash off down the road, which is highly dangerous for him and anyone else he might meet on the way.

The field gate must have a strong padlock on it and a chain, making it thoroughly secure, so that he cannot get out and only you, with the key, can get in. Remember, think safety at all times and you and your pony will be safe. Also remember that if your horse lives in a field he will need company to keep him happy and well.

12
Safety before and at the show

Preparing to ride at a show is one of the most exciting times for a rider but it is also a time when mistakes can be made. When the pressure is on and you are running late there will be a tendency to take short cuts, to make up lost time. Never do this, even if it does mean that you arrive at the show late for one of the classes; hurrying can cause problems and it is better to miss out on an event than hurt yourself or your horse through haste.

If you do everything slowly and methodically, you will not forget anything and will arrive at the show less flustered and, as a result, enjoy it all the more. There is nothing worse than hearing and seeing people who cannot relax or organize themselves because eventually it reflects on the horse in their charge. If the owner is in an unpleasant mood, or angry with himself or someone else, the horse will suffer. He will get the blame for anything that goes wrong and you do not want to be like that.

The way to make life safer for yourself and your mount is to plan everything beforehand, then your day will commence like clockwork and continue in a pleasant vein all the way through.

To begin with, if you are intending to ride at a show, make a note on paper of everything you will require when you get there and when you put each item in the horsebox, or trailer, tick each one off your list. In this way you will not run the risk of leaving anything behind. All it takes on your part is a little organization, thought, and the ability to keep calm when everyone else is making errors and forgetting what they should be doing next.

When you have packed everything away it is time to load your pony or horse. If he does not like going into a box or trailer, remember to allow yourself plenty of time. If he does not like walking up the ramp, do not become frustrated – never shout or wave your arms about at him. That will only frighten him and the chances are he will not go into the box at all. It takes time and a great deal of patience on your part, otherwise you may ruin your pony as far as travelling is concerned.

If he refuses to walk up the ramp right away, try and coax him by talking to him and patting him on the neck. This might give him the extra confidence he needs to walk in. Upset him by shouting or waving a broom at him and he will not want to go into the box or trailer ever again. The best attitude to adopt is one of patience and kindness. Never be too firm and, should you feel like losing your temper, take a deep breath and keep calm.

If you and the horse or pony become upset, accidents may occur; to be safe you must go about things in the correct way. Frighten your horse while trying to load him up, and he could run back off the ramp and step on your feet or, even worse, fall over on to you. Before actually trying to put him in the box or trailer, walk him round the vehicle first and allow him to have a good look at it. Then walk him up to the ramp and, if he stops when his forefeet are on it, give him a pat and talk to him. Even feed him a little tit-bit as a sweetener, and have a hay net hanging in the trailer where he can see it.

If he has a habit of walking off the side of the ramp, park the vehicle alongside a wall so that there is only one side that he can leap off, and have that covered by friends so that it looks to him as though there is only one way to go, and that is forward, into the trailer. Warn your friends, though, to be ready to get out of the way if he starts to play up.

Some horses are really frightened of going up a ramp. If your horse shies away when he sees one, try putting a layer of straw over it and you will probably find that he walks up the ramp without any trouble. But remember, patience is a virtue in this situation, so do everything slowly and calmly.

Some horses and ponies are frightened of going from daylight into the dark of a box. This is understandable, so make sure the vehicle is parked to the best advantage so that daylight is allowed into

Never rush him

the area where he is going to stand.

To protect him during the journey, your mount should be wearing leg bandages and a tail bandage, but these must not be too tight, because if they are they will harm him. The moment you get to the show the tail bandage must be removed. There have been cases in the past where people have put tail bandages on too tight and left them on for too long causing irreparable damage to the tail through loss of circulation. Never let that happen.

Among the items you must always take with you to a show are food and water for your mount. You might be able to buy refreshments there for yourself but not for him so you must provide what he needs. Also have a net of hay in your provisions.

Apart from food supplies you should also have a basic first aid kit with you, so that you can take care of any small cuts or bruises your mount might sustain during the day. It all seems like an awful lot to organize, and it is, but you must stick to the rules of horse ownership. In this way you will not go too far wrong and you will be a lot safer than you otherwise might be.

Also, if you have friends who love horses and ponies, yet cannot afford one of their own, ask them to come along to help you at the show. It will give them something constructive to do, give them a feeling of belonging, and you will find they are extremely useful helping to unload all your tack and belongings at the show. It is always a good policy, too, to have a friend on hand to hold the animal for you if you need to change or dash off to the loo. But do not treat your helpers like slaves – always appreciate their help and say so.

Once you arrive at the show the first job is to unload your pony or horse and make sure he is as comfortable as you can make him. It is going to be a long day for you both and you do not want to start it in the wrong frame of mind. If your journey has been fairly long, put your horse's bridle on and take him for a walk to stretch his legs. Do not put a saddle on him immediately and expect to go galloping all over the place. He will be stiff and the last thing he wants is to be asked to dash about the moment he leaves the trailer or horsebox.

When you have walked him out, tie him by the headcollar to a loop of string on the box and give him a grooming with the body brush, to smarten him up after the journey, and also offer him a drink. Do not give him too much, though, because he will not want to compete with masses of water swilling around inside his tummy. Give him enough for him to be comfortable.

You will have given him his breakfast before you set out, and in my opinion it is best to wait until after you have finished working him to give him his late food. If you were to allow him to eat too much during the day while at a show, when he is jumping or cantering and galloping, it might upset his stomach and you do not want that. A few pony nuts to keep him happy will not do any harm and a net of hay for him to pick at during the homeward journey will settle him down until you arrive safely back at the stables.

When you have groomed him, put his saddle and bridle on and give him some walking exercise around the field where the show is taking place. There are two reasons for this. He will need the ridden exercise after his journey to limber up, and he will also need to get used to the surroundings. This procedure helps to build your mount's confidence, and yours as well. Let him have a good look at what is going on around him, let him experience the different smells and views and do not go everywhere at a gallop. If you do, you are showing off and everyone will know at once that you are inexperienced and not the great rider you think you are. Take things easy and give yourself and your mount time to acclimatize.

There is nothing better for a horse or pony than to feel content and happy with what he is doing. He wants to know what is going on and will be happy with a change of scenery.

Remember that a show is not over in five minutes and you can expect to be there for several hours, so to tire him out mentally and physically within the first hour is inexcusable. Plan the day and take everything calmly and reasonably. One of the biggest dangers at a show is someone who gallops about like a mad thing; the chances are they are heading straight for an accident. There are nearly always lots of people and other animals about and you must not go careering into them.

You will find the biggest problem you face at a show or gymkhana is the number of classes available to you. Do not enter too many because that will not do you or your mount any good. Only enter what you consider is good for you both and do not go pot-hunting and try to win as many rosettes as you can. That is not important, although at the time you might consider it is. The way to treat the whole exercise is to think that you are lucky to own a pony and very lucky to be at the show. It is one thing to be good at riding in competition and another just to go out for everything you can get. You will notice people whose names keep popping up in every class – well, do not follow suit. Your first priority is to make sure that your pony is happy with what he is doing and I can assure you he will not be if he is being asked to gallop and jump all the time. He needs rest, just as you do.

If you do not think you are up to jumping a particular course, do not attempt it, because it will only prove dangerous. You have to know what you are capable of doing and not be led astray by friends who merely want to see you perform so that they can show you off to others. The only way to build confidence is to look, learn, listen and know what your capabilities are. Too many youngsters are pushed too far too quickly, do not enjoy what they are doing and rapidly become disenchanted with the whole joy of riding. Do not let this happen to you. Be firm on this point because you are the only one who knows exactly how you feel. If you think a class is over-extending you, or there is any doubt in your mind that the obstacles are too difficult for your mount to negotiate properly, leave well alone and go for something else.

Once in the arena do not take any notice of anyone outside, just concentrate, make sure you know exactly where you are going and the course you have to take, and carry on with the job in hand. If you try to listen to shouts and instructions from people outside, your concentration will be broken and you will make a mess of what you are doing. You will make mistakes and heighten the chances of your falling off, or your mount refusing. Those on the outside are always full of good intentions and are only trying to help but, believe me, it is far better to make up your own mind about your course of action than to rely on someone shouting instructions when they have their own feet firmly planted on the ground.

By all means discuss tactics before you go into the ring. And, whatever else you do, make sure you walk the course properly. But, once you are mounted and inside the ring, it is your responsibility to see that everything goes according to plan. If you happen to make a mistake, or take the wrong course, do not let it worry you too much because even the best in the world make mistakes. Put it all down to experience and try not to make the same error again.

When you have finished jumping and leave the arena loosen your mount's girths and offer him a drink of water. Never stay on his back trying to impress everyone, because he will become tired and that is totally unfair. When you have completed a class get off his back and lead him about to cool him off. Put his requirements before your own always.

If you only ride in a couple of classes, and do not need your horse or pony for a time, do not tie him up in his box or outside and simply leave him. If it is a brilliantly sunny day he will be terribly uncomfortable standing in the sun all the time unable to move properly. Take care of him at all times and make sure that he has enough water, exercise and plenty of lead-rein walking. His day needs to be made interesting just like yours.

When you have finished at the show, load up all your belongings and tick them off in your notebook as you do so. Then you will not leave expensive equipment behind. Even if you have friends with you it is your responsibility to ensure everything has been loaded into the box and put away safely. On the way back home remind the driver to take it easy so that your horse or pony is not thrown about in the trailer or box. It is amazing how many people, once a sporting function is over, want to get home as quickly as they possibly can. It may be a natural reaction, but your mount, who will be tired, does not want a rough journey, and going too fast or too quickly round bends can make a trip awful for him, if not dangerous. Although you will be tired you must make sure that your horse is travelling well, even if that means stopping on the journey back to check that everything is all right with him. It only takes a few minutes and making that check will give you peace of mind.

When you arrive back at the stables, take him to his box and give him another examination to see that all is well and he has not cut or injured himself in any way. It only takes a few minutes yet you would be surprised how many people just go straight to the stable, let him loose and walk off without a second thought. Do not behave in this manner.

When your mount comes back from a day out, his bed should be already set fair and any droppings picked up and taken away to the muck hill. He will need two buckets of fresh water and his regular evening feed.

By this time you will be exhausted and wishing you could get off back home and have some dinner, a bath, and go to bed. But there are still things to do, so forget that for the moment until your horse has been attended to. One of the jobs you must complete is the foot check. This is to be sure that his shoes are still on properly and to clean out any mud or rubbish that may have collected during the day. When you have picked out his feet, wipe his hooves with a water brush and then apply a dash of hoof oil.

Also, check his dock (under his tail) to see he is not suffering from a sore bottom. If he sweated up during the day you will find that he did so in that area and if you are not careful his dock can become sore. So, using warm water and a clean sponge, carefully and gently wipe away any sweat marks. If he is sore make sure you apply a dash of cream to the affected areas so that he will go through the night comfortably. You know what it is like to suffer from soreness and you also know that your mother will look after you. Well, you must do the same for your horse or pony.

Having fed him and changed the water in his box, give him a hay-net and leave him to relax for the rest of the evening. If he lives out, do all the same checks, ensure that all is well, and then turn him out for the night.

When this has been done there is still a lot of hard work on the agenda, because you have to collect together all the equipment that you used at the show. But, instead of staying on at the stables when, by this time it may be getting dark, ask your parents to come to the yard and give you a lift home. You do not want to be struggling with a saddle, bridle and a range of other items on the bus. Better still, if a friend at the stables has a car, ask them to give you a lift home. Never, of course, accept a car ride from a stranger because that could prove dangerous.

When you have arrived safely home it is time to clean your saddle and bridle. There is no point in putting this job off because it will still be there when you wake up the next day.

Take any bandages that you have used and soak them in a bucket of water or, even better, ask your mother if she will wash them in the washing machine for you. That will make a better job of it and cuts down your workload. If your mother objects about horsey things being cleaned in the machine, you will have to wash everything by hand and hang them out to dry.

When you have finished your cleaning, if you have to leave your tack in the garage make sure you lock the door because, if you do not, you might have your tack stolen. And do not think that because you live in a nice area it will not happen because it might. Saddles and bridles cost a lot and, if they are not insured, are very expensive to replace. If they are stolen it means that you will not be able to replace them right away and that will ruin your riding plans. So lock up the garage.

By now you will feel very tired and dirty and will probably not have eaten properly since you left home. The first thing to do is go and have a bath and a change of clothes. Then have your dinner. But remember that your mother might not share your love of horses and although she goes out of her way to help, she probably will not appreciate you dumping a load of smelly clothes on her when she is tired after a long day. So be pleasant and appreciative and offer her all the help you can and, above all, do not take her, or anyone else, for granted.

If you are old enough, you should be doing your own washing anyway and if you are not, make sure your mother knows that you are grateful she is helping you out. Having parents' backing and help, even if they do not like or understand horses, is a great asset, so do not try their patience by being silly or over-demanding.

13
All about rugs

To save money, and to keep your horse safe in the winter months, you should make sure that some time in the summer you give your New Zealand rugs a complete overhaul. If you neglect them they will not be able to do their job properly when you need to use them again.

A New Zealand rug is used on a horse who is turned out in the winter, and acts as a shield, protecting your mount from the frost, wind, rain and snow. But if holes appear in the waterproof canvas, the rug is next to useless and your horse or pony will suffer.

That is why, when the rug is no longer in use in the late spring (if the weather has turned warm by then), you must give it a good cleaning. You may not want to do it but, believe me, it is worth the effort and will save you a lot of money. It is also the correct thing to do.

The New Zealand rug is made up of waterproof canvas on the outside, with a woollen part-lined blanket underneath. There are chest straps and hind leg straps which cross over and prevent the rug slipping from the animal's back. If your horse hates leg straps, it is possible to buy a rug without them.

If you take the New Zealand home to clean, it is a good idea to use the garage area so that, after sweeping the floor, you can spread the rug out on the ground. Put it down so that the heavy canvas back is on the floor with the woollen blanket facing you. Then, using a stiff brush, get to work on the blanket, removing all the horse hairs and whatever else is sticking to it. When this has been done, mix up a shampoo in warm water and wash the wool as vigorously as you can.

After rinsing the blanket thoroughly, allow to dry properly in the sun. If the weather changes while you are washing the rug, hang it over a pair of step ladders in the garage and give it plenty of time to dry. This could take several days, so be prepared to wait.

When the blanket lining has finally dried, start work on the canvas side, again using the clean floor, but this time putting an old sheet underneath it to protect the blanket. When you have spread the rug out so that no part of it is crinkled and hard to get at, clean off all the mud on the canvas and the leather straps with a stiff brush. Then, again using warm water, apply plenty of elbow grease and wash the canvas until it is clean. When this has been done allow the rug plenty of time to dry.

Then begins the most interesting part of the exercise, because it is now that you can start to apply the reproofing liquid. This can be bought from any camping shop or saddle shop and costs very little. You will also need a paint brush about two inches wide, which you use to paint the reproofer on to the canvas of the New Zealand rug. This is a job which takes time and it must be done properly, otherwise you will miss patches of the rug. Paint a section of the rug at a time and when you have finished one square, have a rest then go on to the next, until the whole canvas area has been painted with the reproofer. Then hang the rug over the step ladders and allow to dry. Do not worry about the reproofer dripping because it soaks into the canvas almost the moment you have put it on, and so you should not make the garage floor messy. When you have hung the rug over the ladder, make sure that you apply saddle soap to all the leather straps to keep them supple and in good order. You do not want the leather cracking.

If your New Zealand rug is old and worn you might find that there is a tear in the canvas which needs repairing. Well, if someone at the stables has one they have cut up for repairs, ask if you can have some of it, and cut a piece out a little larger than you actually need. Then clean the piece of canvas, apply a proprietary glue and stick it over the hole. If you find this impossible to do, then you must take the rug to a saddler to be repaired professionally. It does not cost a lot of money and it will save you having to buy a new rug the following winter.

When you have the New Zealand clean and repaired fold it up the best you can and store it away in a dry place until you want to use it again. As these rugs cost anything between £30 and £60, it pays to keep them in good order. If you can afford it, have two New Zealand rugs so that if one gets wet, you have a replacement.

The point to remember is that if you do not mend a rug that is damaged, if you put it back on your horse or pony again and it has holes in it, the animal will be exposed to rain and other weather hazards. And you know that if he gets cold and wet it could lead to his becoming ill.

It is important that you know exactly how to put the rug on your horse and that is not as easy as many people think. For a start they are much heavier than ordinary rugs and, therefore, much harder to handle for those of you who are not very big. That is why you have to be very careful when you are trying a New Zealand rug on your horse for the first time; when the material, which is completely strange to him, lands on his body, it can sometimes make him nervous. Even if he dances about with fright, do not panic; just take things easy and keep on talking to him and reassuring him that everything is fine. Do not leap back and drag the rug off again because that will make him terrified. And, if he continues to leap about, he might jump on you.

Put the rug on by slowly placing it over the wither area and then, going with the lie of the hairs, pull it slowly, and as quietly as you can, back over the saddle patch to the tail area, so that the end of the rug is just resting over the part where his tail begins.

When you have done this stand back and have a good look at the rug and see where it is creased and needs straightening out. Do everything slowly and methodically and try to get it right first time. The one thing a nervous horse or pony does not want is someone fiddling about with him. Adjust the rug but avoid standing directly behind him to pull it back.

Some people suggest that you should always stand behind the horse for this particular job, but I am against this at any time. The fact is being right behind a horse who is having a rug put on him for the first time is asking for trouble; it would be more sensible if you just stand to one side. It only takes a horse or pony a few seconds to kick out and you could be on the end of the blow. He might not even mean it if he is frightened, but that does not stop the force of the kick smashing one of your legs or badly hurting your face.

Once you have straightened out the New Zealand rug and have it just as you want it, go to the front of the horse and fasten the buckle. Then place the surcingle over the animal's back (if it is not already attached) so that it is hanging down on the offside (right). Then go under the FRONT of the horse and make sure that the roller is hanging properly. Once you have found out that it is, return to the nearside of the animal by the same route.

Then bend down and take hold of the roller and pull it gently toward you and fasten the straps as you would a saddle girth. Do not do them up tightly – just apply enough pressure so that the horse knows exactly what is going on, but does not become frightened. It is, at this stage, all a question of gaining his confidence so that he gets used to having a New Zealand rug on his back.

After you have done this it is time to do up the leg straps which, instead of passing round each hind leg, in fact cross over, the front clips being fastened on the far side of the pony in front of the hind leg. There is a very good reason for the straps to be attached in this way: if they simply went round each hind leg they could press up against them and cause soreness.

Not many horses or ponies object to the rug being on but if one does then you must, for his safety, be very patient and under-standing, until he does accept it without question. When you are absolutely sure that he is not frightened by the weight of the New Zealand rug, or the presence of the leg straps, you can turn him out with one on and have no worries. It is all a question of doing things correctly and in an orderly fashion. Once this has been achieved and his fears have been conquered, he will be safe and will stay warm and dry in cold and wet weather.

Having said that, however, you must always make sure that you check on your mount, preferably twice a day, when he has been turned out in the field with a New Zealand rug on; even though the straps and the surcingle should keep everything in place, sometimes it does not work out like that and the canvas, once he has rolled, ends up hanging awkwardly from his back. If you discover this has hap-pened, you must straighten the rug out again. If you left it hanging, he might get caught up in it and tear the canvas or, even worse, become entangled in it.

Horses and ponies love to roll and mess about in general, that is part of their enjoyment in life, and they do not understand that you have spent time fitting their New Zealand rug correctly so that they can live out. Keep a watchful eye on things so that your horse does not get himself into trouble.

Having dealt with the New Zealand rug, it is time to learn about other kinds of rug, and what they are used for, because they all have their role to play and if you understand that, it could save you problems. Your horse will also be that much safer because of your knowledge.

The first one I will deal with is the anti-sweat rug, which is an absolute boon for those with mounts who tend to sweat up at the mere mention of work. Those mounts who do sweat a lot must be looked after because when they are hot and bothered that is the time they are more likely to catch a chill if you do not do something about it. This is where the anti-sweat rug comes in because it has been specifically designed with hot (sweaty) horses and ponies in mind. These rugs are made of an open cotton mesh, are easy to handle and are very easy to wash and keep clean.

The way to use this particular rug to the best advantage is to rub the horse down with straw, or a stable rubber and then place the light sweat rug over him so that it covers him from withers to the top of his tail. The light mesh will keep him from getting cold, but will still allow enough air to circulate to make him feel comfortable. Race-horse trainers use this type of rug when their horses have finished racing and they have sponged them down and want to walk them around and dry them off. These are also the rugs you see stable staff putting on the horses when they are standing in the unsaddling enclosure, waiting to be led back to their stables. The rugs are light, do a good job and you would be wise to have one available.

When you have finished using the anti-sweat rug always take it home and wash it, then return it to the stables where you keep your tack. These rugs do not take very long to dry because, basically, there is very little to them, so keep them clean and ready to be used when you want them.

In the old days when a horse had finished his work and was very hot, the owner/rider/trainer would use an ordinary rug on his mount, which rested on a layer of straw, placed underneath it to allow the air to circulate. This also enables the horse to dry off, but nowadays anti-sweat rugs have mostly taken over, although straw can still be used when the horse has been out in the rain. Anti-sweat rugs are much easier to handle and you do not finish up with a mount whose back is covered with bits of straw stuck to dried sweat. The light anti-sweat rug is the answer and it has proved beyond doubt that it does what it was designed to do.

These rugs are also useful when you have shampooed your horse or pony in preparation for a show and have rinsed him off and want to dry him. Just pop the anti-sweat rug over his back and walk him around until he is completely dry. Remember, however, you should never give your mount a thorough wash if the weather is very cold, for obvious reasons.

In the winter, if your horse is stabled, he will require a night rug to keep him warm. Night rugs are usually made of jute lined with a woollen blanket. A jute rug may have a stitched on surcingle or you can use a roller to keep it in place. I would recommend that if you do use a rug with a surcingle, you make sure you put a pad over the horse's back under the strap, to prevent it from pressing down on the animal's spine. If you do not do this the surcingle could make him sore and he will become very uncomfortable. Again, it is just a matter of thinking everything out.

It is much better to secure a rug with a roller because it has special padding, which rests either side of the horse's spine and, therefore, prevents pressure. For a horse who has a tendency to become cast (stuck against the wall of his box when rolling) there is a special roller with an arch attached to it, which enables the animal to lie down but not to roll over and so get stuck.

The big trouble with jute rugs is that you may find it difficult to clean them properly; many dry cleaners refuse to put them in their machines. If this is the case in your area, then all you can do is sponge off lightly the worst of the stable stains and thoroughly brush the blanket lining. Then give the rug a good airing before putting it away for the summer.

Rugs made of machine washable materials, usually quilted, are becoming popular nowadays. The only trouble is your horse could possibly be allergic to nylon, in which case you might be well advised to stick to the jute rug.

Also fairly new on the market are rugs filled with polystyrene beads which retain the heat and keep your horse warm in the winter. This type of rug is also machine washable, very easy to handle, dries quickly and is lightweight. That, too, can be an important consideration.

If you are keeping your horse on a tight budget, then a day rug is rather a luxury item and one it is really possible to do without. The alternative during the day is to remove the underblanket, if you are using one, and use the jute rug with the front buckle undone and the fronts turned back and secured under the roller at the withers. Otherwise you could forever be buying two of everything and running up the costs of keeping your horse or pony. With a bit of thought and, in some cases, improvisation, you can then make ends meet without getting into financial difficulties.

Summer sheets are a useful, but not essential, addition to your horse's wardrobe. They are usually made of cotton and should be secured with a surcingle, or roller, and should have a fillet string fitted. This string, which is attached either side of the back of the rug, stops it blowing about in the wind. But remember, when you have put this sheet on, to make sure you pull the horse's tail out from under the fillet string.

When riding in the rain on a horse who will have to be rugged up when he returns to the stable, it is useful to have a rain sheet to put under the saddle, which will keep the horse's back dry. This sheet is also fitted with a fillet string for the same reasons. If you do bring a horse back into its stable wet, you must not just rug him up and leave him because he could easily catch a chill. The way to overcome this is to 'thatch' him. This means putting a layer of straw (or even unwholesome hay which you will not be able to feed him) along his back and then put a rug on inside out over the top. In this way he will dry quickly. If straw is not available, just use a rug inside out; but use a spare one, not the one you want him to wear that night.

Having bought all this expensive wardrobe for your horse, it is essential to look after it well, and that means not throwing items in a corner of a garage, or tack room, when they are not being used. All rugs should be washed or cleaned when not in use and, when well aired, should be folded and stored with moth balls, preferably in polythene bags. When you need them again, remove them from these bags in good of time, and air them to remove the mothball smell.

At this stage you might be thinking that all the equipment I have mentioned is terribly expensive and you cannot see how you could possibly afford everything that goes with owning horses and ponies. To a degree that is correct but, like everything else, you must plan and budget for essentials and add to your horse's equipment as you go along.

The best thing to do is to save up your pocket money before going into horse or pony ownership and that way you will be able to spend the cash on the things your mount needs.

And you must always remember that it pays to buy the best, not because it looks better, but for the simple reason that good quality items are more than likely to last that much longer.

The priority is your horse's health and safety and you will find that if you do not think ahead, and plan everything down to the last detail, you might create problems which could have been avoided.

So when buying rugs always shop around for the best value. Even barter with tradespeople if necessary to get what you want at a price you can afford. There are always bargains to be had, it is just a matter of your going out and finding them.

In the winter you need good clothes to keep warm, and so does your horse. To be safe and sure of his continuing good health buy the best you can afford for him and you will not regret it.

14
Choosing a riding school

Your search for a good riding school will be governed to a great extent by the area in which you live, but if you are to be safe, and be taught the correct way of doing everything, you might have to be prepared to travel. There is no point in attending a riding school if it does not have qualified staff to teach you how to ride properly. First lessons are the ones you generally remember forever, and if those who are doing the teaching do not know their job properly, there will be problems for you at a later date. So be safe and sure.

Before attending a riding school go and watch the people who are already there on rides and see how they are turned out. If they are allowed by the person who owns the school to ride dressed in jeans and wellingtons, find somewhere else. Equally, watch out for the condition of the horses themselves and if they are poor looking, and have straw marks or dried mud caking their coats, stay away from that particular school.

If those concerned cannot be bothered to look after their horses in the way they should be looked after, and are, perhaps, giving them too much work, they will be of no use to you and any time or money spent with them would be a waste. If the local stable you want to attend cannot be bothered to do things properly, forget it and go somewhere else.

That may mean calling upon your parents to give you a lift out of your area, but far better to put them to a spot of bother than support a school which has no right to have a licence. The point to remember is that if the people at a particular stable cannot look after themselves, their clients or their horses and ponies, why should they make

an exception where you are concerned? If they are slovenly in attitude, they will not take the time to teach you to ride properly. They
will cut corners, and are in the business simply to make as much
money as they can, at everyone else's expense. Keep well clear of
riding establishments like this. Even when you find one that does
care, you are still entitled to complain if you feel that not enough
attention is being given to you. You are paying, remember, and
they must provide a suitable and constructive service.

Always be polite, and if you have a point to make, think about it
first and present it in the proper manner. If you are right, there will
be no argument and you will get what you pay for.

In 1982 the Council of the British Horse Society decided that a
.new system for investigating complaints against riding schools
should be established. After this was discussed at length, a panel
of specialists was set up in October of that year. Each of the repre-
sentatives on the panel is a knowledgeable horseman or woman with
experience of running a yard. Nominations to this panel were indi-
vidually approved by the Chairman of the relevant British Horse
Society National Committee. The inspection panel comprises (at the
time of writing) just under forty people, who live in places as far
afield as Inverness in Scotland, Bodmin in the west and Ashford in
Kent to the south east. They have the whole of Britain covered and
are doing a fine job looking after our interests and that of the horses
in this country.

Initially, all were given a thorough briefing by the BHS National
Equine Welfare Officer, and by the BHS National Riding Schools
Inspector on the accepted interpretation of the requirements of the
Acts governing riding schools, and on the standards required. That
was, and is, essential, because everyone knows exactly what is
needed and can take action if they think it necessary.

In the British Horse Society's annual report in September of
1983, it was discovered that a total of 114 complaints had been
received and yet that number was 42 down on the previous year.
That was understandable because not too many people were aware
at that time that the new procedure had been put into operation. Of
the 114 complaints, 57 were found to have been justified and 17
required only advice from the visiting representative. Forty had to
be referred to the licensing authorities for further action. In one

instance there was a prosecution, to which a guilty plea was submitted.

There were several cases where riding schools were refused licences on the expiry of the one they held, or were granted provisional ones until improvement of their establishments had been confirmed. Others were found to have been operating without a licence. It has always been the Society's aim to work towards the creation of higher standards, and the prevention of cruelty or neglect, and they must be given all the help they need.

Without a body like this the whole scene could change; one must always be aware that if standards are allowed to fall horses and ponies in riding establishments could suffer. But if people are aware that should they step outside the guide lines, and behave in a wrongful manner, they might find themselves in trouble, it does at least make them think twice about doing something silly.

Depending on the area in which you live, riding lessons can differ enormously in price and you need to shop around and find the best tuition for the best price. Broadly speaking it is like everything else, and you will usually find that the more expensive establishments will have more highly qualified staff and, therefore, offer better tuition.

Prices can differ, too, depending on whether you want individual tuition or are prepared to be taught with several other beginners. The former is advisable for two reasons. One, because you are getting the instructor's undivided attention, and two, because you will be less embarrassed when you make the inevitable mistakes. Some people do not mind this at all, while others are put off if they think somebody might be laughing at them, or think they are silly because they cannot grasp what is required immediately.

It is up to the individual, but if you think you need lots of time and, perhaps, everything explained to you more than once, then personal tuition is that much better. But remember, the instructor or instructress does not expect you to be brilliant – that is the whole point of your having lessons; they would rather start with you from the beginning so that they do not have to tell you to forget any bad habits you might have picked up before.

The key to successful, safe and enjoyable riding is correct teaching from the start; if you do not understand how things should be done, you will make mistakes, be unhappy and probably give up riding.

The object is to listen and learn as much as you can and be determined to become a good rider by hard work and dedication. Go into riding in a half-hearted manner and you will be unhappy.

You must have a total interest, be consumed with curiosity and eager to learn about safe riding. Anyone can make a mess of things and anyone can be useless where horses and ponies are concerned. Do not let yourself down. Think about what you are doing, listen and learn.

You can pay anything up to about £7 a lesson, depending on where you live. What is particularly important is the type of instructor you get; life in the saddle can be fun, or so difficult that you will wish you had not started riding in the first place. Most instructors, however, are understanding and will give you their time and patience until you know exactly what you are doing.

If you do not like the riding school in your area, the thing to do is to travel out of your town or village until you find a place that suits you. Having British Horse Society approval does not always mean that a school is better than one that is not approved. But if it has the stamp of approval of that particular organization, it can almost be guaranteed that it will suit your needs, and that includes qualified instruction. Any riding school which has been approved by the British Horse Society will have a plaque displayed somewhere. It is not something people hide away.

Qualified instructors will have spent years training and passing exams so that they know exactly what they are doing, have the safety of you and the horses you are riding uppermost in their minds, and know how to handle any given situation. That is not to say that someone who has not had BHS training would not know as well, it just means that those who have will possess certificates to prove it.

Another thing to remember when you are looking for a riding school to go to is the state of the stable yard. If it is dirty and has barrows and forks strewn about the place, particularly in mid-afternoon, I would think twice about staying there. The yard should be nice and tidy, with equipment put away in the proper places – there is no excuse for mucking out tools to be on display at three in the afternoon. That is a sign of slackness and an open invitation to accidents, particularly if clients have to mount their horses in the yard. Your mount could step on a fork or shovel, or bump into a wheelbarrow that should not be there. And when there are inexperienced riders trying to learn how everything should be done, it is not setting them a good example. It also indicates a lack of organization.

Before you begin riding lessons at a school, also spend time there watching how the staff prepare the horses and ponies for riding. Before any mount is taken from its stable, the animal should have had its feet picked out; if it has not, it is a sign of laziness. When you have enough experience you will be able to do this yourself, but there should be grooms and helpers who know what they are doing to make sure the horses' feet are free of mud and stable waste.

The responsibility for all the horses at a riding school is the proprietor's, and he or she should make sure that the staff are doing the job correctly; if they are taking short cuts, they should lose business. Nobody deserves to be paid for something that is not being done properly and efficiently. You are the person who is paying for lessons, and you have the right to go elsewhere if you are not satisfied.

The animals should be groomed properly and their tack must be in good order. The latter is a very important point because saddles and bridles that have not been looked after become unsafe. The bridle should not have sweat marks over it, and the saddle should be cleaned and polished. There are no excuses for dirty tack and if the riding school you are attending ever presents you with a mount wearing a dirty, sweat-encrusted bridle, complain and insist that the tack is changed at once. Also think twice about returning to such a place.

As I have already explained, if the leather of a bridle is not kept clean, it weakens and cracks and could break while you are riding, in which case you will lose control of the horse or pony. This could lead to you falling off and being injured and the horse charging off out of control and hurting other, innocent people. All because someone could not be bothered to spend the time looking after their tack properly.

When checking out your riding school, which you have every right to do, make a note of how many times a certain horse or pony is taken out each day. Some mounts are overworked and that is not good for them or their riders because, like an athlete who overtrains, the edge is taken off their performance and they are not as good as they should be. There is nothing more off-putting than riding a horse who is fed up with what he is doing, because of over-use. And nothing is more guaranteed to put a youngster off riding than to be mounted on something that resembles a working machine, rather than a warm, living creature who wants to please. It is also totally unfair on the pony or horse, and you do not want to take part in overuse or abuse of animals.

Another important factor to keep in mind when searching for a riding school is to make sure there is somewhere safe for you to ride. Some establishments are very lucky in that they have green belt land nearby, with bridlepaths and fields, which they can use when they like. The approach to such places will be free of heavy traffic and you will not have to ride a great deal on roads. When you are inexperienced, the less riding you have to do on roads the better, because you will be cutting down the risk of accidents. Sometimes riding on roads is unavoidable, but there is a vast difference between riding on a minor road and having to contend with a great deal of traffic on a major one. Many horses and ponies are used to cars, lorries and buses, but it can be off-putting for the young, inexperienced rider, particularly if the weather is bad, and their hands and feet are freezing or soaking wet and they are riding a pony who would rather be back in the stable yard than trundling, bedraggled, around roads.

Indeed, you should not be sent out on roads when you are first learning to ride. Any establishment that suggests you should join a ride, when you cannot even sit straight in the saddle or trot properly, is one to steer clear of. You will not be totally safe, no matter how good your mount is in traffic.

Having dealt with what you should expect from a riding school, I will now tell you what you should do to help them so that there is never any misunderstanding between you. Never tell a riding school that you are a good rider when you are not. Some people would know as soon as you sat on one of their horses that you were inexperienced, while others might not, and that could lead to trouble for you and the horse or pony. Never try to be clever and always tell the truth. It can be highly dangerous if you tell someone you are a good rider when you are not and they put you, in all good faith, on a mount who is too strong for you. Being run away with is a terrifying experience and if you hardly know the first thing about riding, it is even worse.

When, for some inexplicable reason a horse or pony does bolt, it takes a great deal of know-how, total self-control on the part of the rider and a lot of luck to pull up without either of you being the worse for the experience. Someone who does not know how to keep control of his or her mount or, indeed, themselves in such a situation, could be badly hurt, and nobody wants that, least of all you.

Remember, there is nothing wrong with not knowing how to ride properly; even the best had to start at the bottom. In fact, the best riders never stop learning, even when they have had many years of experience.

It is the greatest feeling of all working a horse or pony with whom you are in total harmony, but when something goes wrong for the inexperienced rider it can be awful. Nobody wants to see you hurt yourself and people in the horse world will go out of their way to help. But what riding school owners and instructors do not appreciate are people who think they know it all when they do not, and are too proud to think a little and learn.

Once you have found the school you want and are satisfied that all is in order, listen to everything the instructors have to say to you and concentrate. In the free period when you are not riding make notes of what has happened during the day and study them in the evening. That will refresh your mind and you can work out where you went wrong, if indeed you did. Bear in mind that you cannot learn to ride in five minutes – there is a lot of effort attached to it all.

Also, read as many good books on the subject as you can; study different methods of doing things and remember the ones that suit you best. It always helps when the person teaching you says something and you know, to a certain degree, what they are talking about. For example, if they say 'Grip with your knees and keep your heels down in the stirrup irons', you do not immediately grip with your heels and plunge your feet downwards. You may think that no one would do that, but in fact they sometimes do, and it makes the instructor's job that much harder. Listen, learn, do what they say and remember what they have said.

If you can, make a point of staying on after your lesson, not only to watch other pupils and the mistakes they make, but to discuss your lesson with your instructor. You will be surprised at what you can learn by such after-teaching discussions, because many instructors will explain exactly what you are doing wrong and the way for you to correct your mistakes. They will also see that you are keen to learn, and that will please them, for there is nothing worse for a teacher to say something one minute and see it forgotten, or disregarded, the next.

It has a knock-on effect as far as relationships go, because there is nothing more pleasing for an instructor than to watch a pupil improving and becoming good at what he or she is doing. They will take more notice of you and be prepared to give you more of their time to help with any problems you may have. And, of course, recognizing a mistake and correcting it leads to safer riding for you.

Like everything else in this world, riding lessons cost money and, before actually going for lessons, you should save up for them so that you are not always asking your parents for money. They might be very willing for you to learn to ride, but many will realize, without being told, that it is an expensive business and will not appreciate it if you keep approaching them for extra cash, which, in many cases, might not be available.

But most of you are given pocket money and what I suggest you do is start a riding fund. When you have managed to save sixty or seventy pounds (and you will be surprised how grandparents and aunts and uncles will chip in) use that for your lessons. That way you will not have to worry about whether you can afford a lesson and, just as important, you will have the benefit of continuity of lessons. There is nothing worse than doing well one week and having to wait another month before you can have the next lesson. Far better to save and know what you can afford, than to keep worrying your parents for more money and wonder if you will be able to meet the costs of the next riding session.

You will soon know if you want to take up riding seriously – it is a feeling that continues to grow within you and an excitement that cannot be dampened down. If you do not feel that way, you must ask yourself whether riding is really just a passing phase. The thing to remember is that riding is expensive and if you intend just to play at it, it would be far wiser to take up some other, less expensive hobby.

But, if you *are* so keen that you get a tingling feeling when you even think about horses and ponies, then nothing in this world will stop you succeeding. Do not, however, imagine that it will be easy, because it will not. You will make many mistakes; but instead of moaning about them and being put off, turn them to your advantage, make sure you do not make them again and you will find you are leading a happy and satisfied life.

So, start to save up for your riding lessons, and do not worry if it seems to take an age, because there will always be riding schools around. Sensible saving will allow you to do the things you want to do without inconveniencing your parents. When you have learnt to ride properly they will have their work cut out ferrying you from one show to the other, so you want to set off in the right direction to start with.

If you are not sure where the approved riding schools are in your area, just write to the British Horse Society at the British Equestrian Centre, Stoneleigh, Warwickshire CV8 2LR, and ask them to send you a list. Remember to enclose a stamped, self-addressed envelope for their reply and be prepared to pay for any literature they send you.

It is also a good move to belong to the Pony Club, because most riding schools are associated with a branch of it and organize pony activities which will be of great benefit to you. Any good riding school will be able to tell you who the district commissioner of your area is and all you have to do is make contact with them.

15
Sensible riding

We are very fortunate in Britain that pedestrians and riders have certain rights of way, where they can walk at their leisure, or ride across country. There are, however, separate paths for those who are on foot, and bridlepaths for those riding horses or ponies and, when mounted, you should never stray on to footpaths. If you are at all unsure where your local bridlepaths are, ask other riders in the locality or go to the library and ask to see an Ordnance Survey Map of the area. Where bridlepaths are clearly marked on the map, nobody can stop you using them: they are there by right.

This does not mean, however, that you can do exactly what you like when using bridlepaths, and make a nuisance of yourself. You must keep your horse to the designated area and use the right of way properly. Time and time again I have seen riders galloping all over the place, not taking any notice whatsoever of the markers on the trees through which the bridlepath runs.

There are several reasons for obeying the law on this matter, not the least of which is safety, not only for yourself but for other people as well. People who go walking enjoy the countryside as much as you, and there is nothing worse for them than to be having a pleasant day in the country with their children, or dogs, and for you to come galloping around a bend at full speed heading straight for them. They might be lucky enough to get out of the way but, on the other hand, there may be an accident and people could be hurt. If you have taken no notice of the restrictions of the bridlepath, you could well be responsible in law for any damage done and that is not good for you – or your parents' bank balance.

Worse than that is the fact that your silly misbehaviour may be the cause of someone being badly injured for ever, in which case you would find it very difficult to forgive yourself. The fact is the markers on the trees have been put there so that you will be able to see at a glance where you are permitted to go, so use them properly and do not stray and spoil other people's pleasure.

You must always remember that although you absolutely adore riding and horses, there are many people who do not; they have rights, just as you do, and you must respect those rights. You will be very tempted, particularly in the winter months when rain and snow have made the bridlepaths sloshy, to skirt around them and stray on to the ground where people walk. But you must resist that temptation otherwise, after a while, that ground, too, will become just as bad; and, even worse, there will be complaints by walkers to the local council and everybody who rides will suffer as a consequence. So stick to the rules and everyone will be happy.

Many of the bridlepaths and walks are, of course, not just in woodland areas, but across fields and, again, you must be aware of what you can and cannot do. Although it is your right to use such trails, some farmers or landowners become angry and feel you should not be there in the first place. It only takes a few silly people to cause a lot of trouble and ill-feeling. It is not unheard of for bridleways to be closed for these reasons. So when you are riding in a field, always stick to the edges of it, particularly at a time when crops are growing, unless, of course, the bridlepath runs elsewhere. And keep your eyes open at all times in case there is machinery on the land, or old bits of tractors that have been abandoned and left to rot. Walking into or standing on bits of metal is the quickest way of making your mount lame, so be aware of the dangers at all times.

It would also be unfair to ignore completely the farmer's rights. You must not destroy all his hard work and his crops by walking straight across the middle of, say, a field full of wheat when the young shoots are just breaking through; or by ploughing a furrow through the middle of a full grown crop. You might think that such things do not happen, but I can assure you they do.

That is one of the reasons why the British Horse Society, and all those connected with the Rights of Way question, have had to work so hard on your behalf for a very long time. They all know how important it is to stick to the rules and it makes it all that much harder for the people who do care if you ignore the rules and do exactly what you like, when you like. Always think of others before yourself and you will be halfway to being a good, considerate rider.

In many of the fields you ride across there will be sheep and cattle; if there are, you must not gallop past them, because this might disturb them. They might then dash about and become too excited or, if it is the lambing season, or the cattle are in calf, their offspring might be damaged. If this happens the farmer could sue you, and rightly so, because he does not want his livelihood threatened. Be careful, walk gently across fields where there are other animals, and the chances are nothing will happen. All it takes is a little thought on your part to make sure that everything goes well.

Access to many of the fields you cross will be through a gate, which you must open and be sure to close again, even if you are in a desperate hurry or your mount is unsettled and being a nuisance. Failure to comply with this simple rule of the country could cause you and other riders a great deal of trouble. The reason is that if you left a gate open, farm animals might get out, or in – one can be just as bad as the other. Suppose the farmer was using rotational grazing, and needed to keep the grass in the field you were in for specific reasons. Then you left the gate open and his sheep or cows in another field wandered in and started munching their way through it. It would completely ruin his plans, and the animals could become very ill through over-eating. So when you open any gate make sure that you shut it again behind you. It may all take a little more time and effort but, even if you are in a dreadful hurry and want to get home quickly, you must still take those extra seconds to close the gate.

There will also be many occasions when a gate, or stile, looks inviting enough to be jumped instead of opened. But resist that temptation because it can be highly dangerous, even if you are riding a horse you know could clear the largest obstacles. The reason for this is that if you were riding out in the country on your own and you tried to jump a gate and your horse blundered and fell, there would be nobody around to help you. If you had a fall and broke an arm or leg, or suffered any other sort of injury, you would be in serious trouble.

Apart from that there is also a chance that your mount might hurt himself and need the attention of a vet. If you were miles from the nearest village that could cause you and the horse a great deal of hardship. Some people might say that hunters jump gates, and other obstacles, and continue to do so even though they know the risks involved. What you must remember is that when you are out hunting there are other people doing the same thing and there are often many people following the hunt in cars and on foot, so that if there is an accident, the chances of help being summoned quickly are much greater.

But when you are having a ride in the country on your own it is a vastly different matter. You must think about safety at all times, even if you consider it is spoiling your fun. Apart from the fact that you might be hurt, there is another important reason for not jumping gates and stiles: there is always the chance that you might break them. You must respect others' property – then farmers and other landowners will not mind you riding on their land.

Another important point to keep in mind is tidiness. Too many people use the country as though it is a dustbin, throwing their rubbish into the nearest field or hedge. It might then be out of sight, but it is not the correct thing to do, and nobody else wants to go around after you clearing up. So keep your sandwich or sweet wrappers in your pocket until you get home and then put them in the waste bin.

If you are going out on a long ride, and wish to take sandwiches and something to drink, carry the drink in a plastic container for safety. Glass bottles can be dangerous, particularly if you fall off. If they shatter, you could cut yourself badly. I have even heard of cases when a bottle has been broken and the rider, who was fortunate enough not to be hurt, has simply left the glass where it was and ridden away. That was very wrong, because other horses or farm animals passing that way could have stepped on to the broken glass and cut themselves. It is not fair to them, or the person who owns them, and your bad habits will put that person off horses and riders. And, if a complaint is made, and the culprit found, there could be a lot of trouble and maybe even a court action.

The best thing to do is not to carry any of your lunch, or tea, in your pockets – that way you will avoid accidents. Just pack your meals in a waterproof bag and tie it securely to the saddle so that it does not flap about, or fall off as you are riding.

One of the biggest problems facing riders in some areas is the lack of bridleways, and other routes suitable for horses. Many local councils do as much as they can as far as this is concerned, because they know how important the matter is. They are also aware that riders need routes in and around towns on which to ride. And, as I have already pointed out, they know that continuous use of the same trails by too many riders can have devastating results on the ground.

This is why it is so important for you to understand that if you do not use the routes available in your area properly, there will be no incentive for the councillors to go out of their way to help you. Doing things in the correct manner is vital, not only for your safety but also to encourage the powers that be to help you. If your local council keeps receiving complaints that riders are untidy, and do not care about anyone except themselves, the case for more and better bridlepaths will be drastically weakened. It is important that riders should try to help themselves on so important a matter. On a local level, you can approach your local council for additional bridleways. Or you could start a bridleways action group and get support from local riding schools and Pony Club branches.

It is such an important matter that the British Horse Society's Bridleways Office at Stoneleigh, in Warwickshire, is continuously involved with matters of national significance in this area. A classic case of their involvement is the matter concerning the re-introduced Dartmoor Commons Bill. In the first Bill the general rights of access granted were confined to pedestrians; but the new bill grants the right of access to those on 'Foot and Horseback'. That was a tremendous achievement on the part of those concerned with the action; but if they had not been around to take the proper steps, would anything constructive have happened for horse and rider?

The BHS office also has much literature on bridleways available to members. This includes 'Policy on Bridleways', 'Policy on Width of Bridleways', 'Reclassification of Roads Used as Public Paths', 'Obstruction of Rights of Way', 'Freedom To Ride' and many other booklets containing all the information you could possibly need.

It is tremendous that there is an equestrian authority to take the time and make the effort to look after our interests, because without that valuable help a lot of important points would be overlooked, and some routes, which could be used by riders, would merely go to waste. This work takes time and money, so when you buy any literature on bridleways you are, in effect, helping the cause, because your cash boosts the funds of those at Stoneleigh who do the research and fight the battles.

My own view is that it is a first-class organization and we should all support it as much as possible. Without it we would find everything connected with the horse that much harder, particularly when it comes to trying to get something worked out with local councils. Some councils are caring, but others are much less so.

Index

Jacqueline McGee

65 Whitehill
Glenisla Cottage